Pastoral Assertiveness

Pastoral Assertiveness

A NEW MODEL FOR PASTORAL CARE

PAUL MICKEY/GARY GAMBLE
with Paula Gilbert

ABINGDON
Nashville

PASTORAL ASSERTIVENESS

Copyright © 1978 by Abingdon

Library of Congress Cataloging in Publication Data

MICKEY, PAUL A. 1937-
    Pastoral assertiveness.
    1. Pastoral theology. I. Gamble, Gary, 1943- joint author. II.
Gilbert, Paula, 1952- joint author. III. Title.
BV4011.M483   253   78-9020

ISBN 0-687-30138-6

MANUFACTURED BY THE PARTHENON PRESS AT
NASHVILLE, TENNESSEE, UNITED STATES OF AMERICA

to
Skip Moore
Sam Hook

ACKNOWLEDGMENTS

We extend our appreciation to our families and all who have directly and indirectly contributed to this project while we sustained classroom and professional responsibilities. Our mutual respect and thankfulness are extended to Mrs. Jacquelyn Norris for her unwavering dedication in deciphering consistently poor handwriting, for her sense of humor in the face of overbearing typing and duplicating demands, and for her grace in working with us throughout the entire project; and to one, Charlie Browne, a warm friend of Viking legend, who quietly and faithfully supported us in this adventure. For his perceptive insights in shaping the final character of this study, we hold Charles K. Morrison in deep professional and personal regard.

Finally, we express our gratitude for those ministers and parishes whose struggles in ministry have become manifestly a part of this study. We trust that only constructive results will follow.

Paul Mickey
Gary Gamble
Paula Gilbert

Durham, North Carolina
November 30, 1977

CONTENTS

PART IV

INTRODUCTION

Among individuals contemplating a career in ministry and for many lay people considering a more active role in their local churches, their widely claimed motivation is often expressed as "I want to help people" or "I want to bear witness to how God has changed my life." The political power struggles of human life inside and outside the church can quickly frustrate a naive and simplistic approach to ministry and thwart the church's mission. What others frequently reject is this unexamined naiveté—not the gospel of Jesus Christ.

Through its ordained and lay ministries the church is called by her Lord to respond to the needs of others. But simple responsiveness is not enough. Out of the ruinous ashes of well-intended theological and humanistic hopes for ministry come the fading and haunting echoes of destroyed plans, crippled careers, and lacerated dreams. A painful chorus from the disillusioned and disappointed may be clearly heard: "What went wrong? Why are people unresponsive to or rejecting of our efforts to help?"

"Active listening" is a valuable experience in training for counseling. In this book we extend this principle to include "active caring." We call it pastoral assertiveness—the informed, responsible way to provide pastoral leadership through care, guidance, and concern and to offer effective help in circumstances where the pastor is called to assume active and assertive caring. Efforts in theological education to develop pastoral sensitivity in listening, accepting, and supporting have been rewarded. A motif in this style of pastoral sensitivity is the ability to place the interactional burden on the other party. "The other" is encouraged to provide the lead and initiative in introducing data and issues for the pastoral conversation. The pastor is trained to support, listen, and clarify. This style of pastoral caring is extremely valuable in crisis-type situations. But it does not suffice for *all* human interactions. It is not responsive to the biblical call to proclaim and thereby, in some direct measure, take initiative in proclaiming the gospel of Jesus Christ in words and deeds of ministry.

Many pastors feel uncomfortable in taking initiative to proclaim the Word and to offer the deed of reconciliation. Such uneasiness flows from over-generalizing training which teaches always to listen, support, reflect, and summarize. In this style of ministry the other party (person, group, or institution) is encouraged to establish, claim, and control its goals.

Ministers are ordained, and laypersons are called to a lively faith that is sensitive in responding to the personal feelings of the other. Active caring implies consciously asserting care for another when decisions need to be made and victories need to be won. Both pastoral responsiveness and assertiveness belong in a pastor's ministry. These modes of relating cannot be separated or polarized into warring camps if the church ministers are to be faithful to the witness of Scripture and the lives of the saints who have preceded them. Many lay people and pastors believe that both gifts of ministry should be more in evidence: pastoral responsiveness *and* pastoral assertiveness.

Many pastors, whose training in pastoral care has been guided by a client-centered or responsive model, experience a sense of failure and feelings of guilt and anger when they are dismissed after attempting to assert their own values, beliefs, and feelings, or otherwise try to provide assertive leadership in pastoral activities. We believe that assertiveness needs to be understood intellectually and self-consciously as a legitimate and constructive aspect of Christian ministry. Brief testimony of battle-scarred clergy and laity indicate that some of the more painful parish conflicts occur in settings where the presence and sheer intensity of pastoral assertiveness is either denied or not acknowledged and therefore is used ineffectively and destructively.

Pastoral responsiveness and pastoral assertiveness for clergy and laity are essential elements in ministry. They go hand in hand, theologically and emotionally. One mode of ministry cannot carry the weight and responsibility of the other.

Chapter 1 illustrates the actual results when pastoral assertiveness is not incorporated with responsiveness in a pastor's ministry. In fact, a struggle to develop a suitable model for pastoral care based on an actual encounter (see "Whose Prime Time?" p. 32, chapter 1) prompted this study.

The minister involved wanted to become more effective in his pastoral contacts. A series of reports were analyzed and progress was in evidence. Then came an incident with a television set. The pastor had made an appointment to visit a home, and a warm invitation was given. When the pastor arrived, however, the actual living-room setting was not conducive to pastoral conversation. The television set controlled the family and any effort at conversation. The blaring TV rendered sensitive relationships hopeless and created a general awkwardness between the pastor and his parishioners.

The pastor's dilemma was apparent but complex. "Do I turn off the set? Do I ask them to turn it off? Do I ask permission to turn it off? Do we pretend it is not there and launch into my purpose for the visit? Do I settle for idle chatter and silent commentary? Do I leave?" How can the pastor have the television set turned off so that conversation and the pastor's intentions may be served?

Paul Mickey had no informed answer for the pastor. None of his theological and professional training or experience had prepared him for this practical question. Not willing to give up and abandon the pastor with such an ethical and psychological dilemma (of how to gain pastoral control in this situation), they agreed, in the midst of mutual frustration, "There has to be a better way! There must be a better way to make pastoral calls."

The frustration became more focused: "Who is trained to turn off the TV in someone else's house?" Perhaps someone in house-to-house sales work would have practical training of this kind.

Paul Mickey called Gary Gamble, a longtime friend. Gary is a seminary graduate and an ordained minister with several years of experience in both large and small churches. He is trained in door-to-door sales for summertime, college employment. It was quickly discovered that sales theory and training time are devoted specifically to the art of turning off living-room television sets. Indeed, many of the practical, everyday problems that frustrate and intimidate clergy in their parish settings are also problems that the "outside" or door-to-door sales representative encounters and must overcome if sales are to be made.

Several conversations led to the conclusion that the dynamics of sales encounters are not substantially different from typical pastoral calling activities. This realization prompted us to develop a new model of pastoral care, a model that was the genesis of this work in pastoral assertiveness. This model would enable clergy to be faithful to the gospel, to be sensitive in listening, and to be assertive in securing decisions that would benefit the persons, groups, congregations, and communities involved in the church's ministry.

About the same time, Paula Gilbert, currently engaged in doctoral studies in church history, enrolled in a pastoral theology course taught by Paul Mickey. This was her first formal exposure to the field of pastoral care and counseling. Classroom lectures and small group discussions further established in her mind the need to offer a model of pastoral assertiveness for parish ministers and for scholars who are trained in the classical disciplines of biblical studies, church history, and systematic theology. As a student of church history, Paula's perception of pastoral care—one generally shared by her colleagues—was that the net result of pastoral training frequently led ministers toward intellectual and liturgical passivity. Thus, many able seminary students avoid pastoral care and counseling fearing personal and professional passivity.

Ministers trained in the classical theological disciplines, frequently experience shell shock upon arrival in the parish and jettison the strength of their training as they initiate desperate efforts to develop the practical skills related to pastoral care. The tragedy is that classical disciplines and pastoral care are seldom reintegrated in a satisfactory manner in the parish. The result is a frustrated ministry of pastoral responsiveness alone. In offering pastoral assertiveness as a model for active caring we hope to avert some of the mistrust between the two areas so that effective, integrated ministry can be accomplished.

Paula accepted the challenge to make a contribution to a revised understanding of parish ministry that asserts truth and ideas as well as engages in crisis intervention. With this in mind, she joined the project to offer a model of pastoral assertiveness that is congenial with principles in pastoral care, scriptural truths, and the historical realities of the church.

That's how it all began. The following pages show where the questions and the various perspectives led.

PART I

CHAPTER 1

CRISIS IN
PASTORAL CARE

Pastoral care is a disciplined effort to offer responsible theological and psychological leadership and assistance to individuals, groups, and organizations. This ministry may be offered in a variety of circumstances, including specialized pastoral psychotherapy or in the general, everyday life of a local church congregation. Actually, all activities of the church's ministry are occasions for pastoral care.

The crisis in pastoral care emerges from an overspecialization focused on the crises of death and bereavement, interpersonal and family conflicts, and critical stages of personality and identity development. In crisis ministry generally, pastoral care is best offered by means of supportive, clarifying, and paraphrasing activities, acts of caring that may be termed *healing* and *sustaining*.

Pastoral care as practiced in crisis intervention typically creates the expectation that explicit guidance and direct answers by the pastor or layperson are not to be entertained. Our thesis throughout this study is that *guidance,*[1] along with healing and sustaining, is an appropriate expression of pastoral care; that the inability to understand and utilize the dynamics of guidance and assertiveness constitute a failure of nerve and ministry; that this crisis of overspecialization and restricted perspective in pastoral care can be overcome in ways that complement healing and sustaining; and, that the current crisis in parish leadership stems from a failure to develop guidance and assertiveness in ministry. Our concern is to help develop a general perspective on guidance as well as to suggest some of the specific dynamics and modes of behavior by which guidance, as pastoral care, may be expressed.

I.
Crisis in Caring

The following cases provide a brief sample of the crises encountered, if not created, by many pastors and local congregations. These problems do not involve viciousness, deceit, ill will, or malicious forethought. Fine and gentle persons of good intention, however, often create disastrous results in their efforts at ministry. Why the unwanted endings and sad conclusions? Why the wrong directions and the needless floundering?

Most crises in pastoral care and parish leadership occur as one of three types: ineffective technique, situational uncertainty, or ego-inhibition.

(1) *Ineffective Technique.* This includes pastors and laypersons who rely excessively upon techniques of caring. These leaders have dull sensitivities and undeveloped egos and therefore grasp at any or all techniques; or, they have developed no techniques whatsoever and are hapless victims of circumstance. In both instances techniques are not used wisely; they are used to excess or the skills needed to relate to people and the ministry of pastoral care are undeveloped.

(2) *Situational Uncertainty.* This involves people (laity and clergy) who will not take charge. Many pastors or laypersons wish to give a valid and valuable expression of Christian ministry. However, their good intention slips from their grasp and someone else takes charge. Uncertainty can turn into a dependency that forces or allows others to establish

leadership and defeats the intent of conscientious caring. Someone else is posing the questions and providing the answers. Pastoral drifting confines pastoral care to hearing feedback, to reflecting and supporting another's desires and sense of direction. The uncertain minister who drifts along fails to offer leadership; someone else takes charge and determines the flow and outcome of the relationship.

(3) *Ego-Inhibition.* Some Christians are afraid to claim a strong identity or self-love. They protest that a strong personal ego would hamper their desire to express God's love and their eagerness to serve others in need. Such self-depreciation destroys the ego strength needed to exercise pastoral care in situations of conflict.

Again, these are the three major problem areas: too much or too little technique; other people dominating the theological and emotional agenda; an inability to claim one's own ego strength and theological integrity in relationships. These three failings illustrate the major components of the crisis in pastoral care.

We have used verbatim materials from actual case studies to illustrate the crisis. Each case has two parts. (1) *The Problem* briefly states the situation and shares an excerpt from a critical segment of pastoral care activity. (2) *The Answer* provides suggestions for alternative ways of handling the situation.

A. *Ineffective Technique*

Techniques exist for accomplishing the pastoral ministries of the church. Lay people likewise, in their areas of specialty, have opportunity to develop techniques that enable them to engage in effective pastoral care. When various techniques for achieving goals come together in a parish setting, internal conflict may be experienced within or between clergy and laity, or it may involve theological, emotional, or group conflict. Conflict emerges when no skilled technique is employed; or, a technique is applied inappropriately and is overextended; or, the technique is used self-consciously to exploit and manipulate others. The following examples illustrate problems in technique.

Scriptural Swamping

The Problem. A laywoman spoke to her pastor about a problem in the Bible study group which she leads.

Linda: Well, . . . it's supposed to be a Bible study, but we don't do much studying.

Pastor: You mean you never get around to using the Bible?

Linda: No, it's just the way we use it. The way we have been doing it is taking a topical approach and using a concordance. We take a topic like marriage and look it up in the concordance and then read all the verses where marriage is mentioned, trying to find out what the Bible says about it.

Pastor: And you don't like this approach?

Linda: This is not Bible study to me. They never use any commentaries. They just want to see what the verses say. But I think you have to understand them in their context. In fact, Norma even said the only way to understand it is just read it over and over, and God will reveal it to you.

At this point the pastor lapses into silence, then diverts the conversation to something else!

The problem involves verse swamping: Norma and her cohorts falsely assume that submergence in Bible verses is Bible study. As Linda perceives the problem, the verses are washing over the group without critical understanding. She demands that scripture verses and passages be considered in context. The pastor fails to address this issue; he provides no guidance or direction in the interpretive techniques that he was exposed to in seminary, nor does he offer support when Linda claims that Bible study has a proper interpretive setting.

The Answer. Here is a problem of too much technique on the one hand, and not enough on the other. Norma and her group are succumbing to ineffective technique by simply staring at verses of Scripture and believing that insight will flow to the group. The pastor is ineffective because he does not provide the critical, constructive response needed. Linda is right, but the pastor is of little help. Commentaries are needed to place the verses of Scripture—whether they regard marriage, eternal life, or funerals—into their larger context and to prevent them from overwhelming the readers. Why does the pastor fail in this situation? Scripture swamping is an entrenched problem that a pastor cannot hope to challenge with a *laissez faire* technique. The pastor fails because he will not assert his leadership by providing a better method of Bible study. He should and probably does know better, but he will not assert himself theologically and emotionally.

Being Set Up
The Problem: Mr. Miller, a successful pastor, recently moved to a new congregation. Soon a distressed and respected member of his previous congregation calls about a problem. The new pastor at the former church has invited a revivalist for a series of services, under pressure of some, but not all, the laity. Some other members of the church protest, feeling manipulated and exploited. Crosscurrents of ineffective leadership rip the situation apart.

Mr. Miller: If some of you would talk to him and let him know that y'all are in support of him, I think

Katherine: Well, that's what I wanted to talk to you about.

Mr. Miller: Ahhhh . . . what?

Katherine: Well, some of us hinted to him that he could maybe spend more time with sermons because some of them are not so good. And . . . ah . . . I thought since you were going to see him tomorrow, you might just say something to him. He seemed kind of offended when we said something to him, but I know he would respect more what you say. I don't know what you could say, but I know you will be able to do something. He seems so down all the time.

Mr. Miller: *(Not knowing what to say.)* Well . . . I don't know . . . I'll see him tomorrow, but I don't know what I'll say. `

Katherine: We tried to talk to him, but he'll listen to you better. I think he'll really appreciate it, coming from you. He really respects you.

Clearly Mr. Miller is at sea, not knowing how to respond. One possible response he fails to express to Katherine is, "No, I can't do it for you. You need to do it yourself." He hints at this response in his initial comment, but he allows the opportunity to pass. Katherine puts the bite on him, and he is reluctant either to affirm that he will say something or to assert that he will not.

The Answer. After remarking upon his good graces and interpersonal gifts, Katherine then puts a question to the pastor which sets him up for the kill—"Don't you think something ought to be done?" Obviously, something should, and the pastor agrees. This is the nibble for Katherine, and she follows with, "Why don't you do it?" The pastor's answer should have been, "I cannot do that for you. It involves your church, your situation, and your new pastor; you will have to negotiate that. I cannot do that for you; I'm sorry." Good counseling technique would reflect to Katherine what she had said without agreeing to do the work for her. But the pastor fails to use that expression of caring and loses control of his own integrity because he cannot say no and mean it.

A Moral Issue

The Problem: Money, cars, and indulgent guardians form the contours of David's life. Earlier in the conversation David moans, "Everything's going wrong at once . . . that stupid car . . . and school . . . and the bank won't give me my allowance early to get my car fixed." He continues listing the abuses and frustrations that come his way. Eventually he turns to the pastor revealing pangs of conscience about his conduct.

David: No, I do not want to hassle them anymore. I have been through that . . . The only person that cares about me is Carolyn (the sixteen-year-old he dates) . . . I guess that is why I really came . . . I love her . . . but I am too old for her . . . I told her I like her a lot, but she says she is too young to make any commitment. . . . But she said that she likes me, too. Helen and George are great (Carolyn's parents). Do you think that I should stop dating Carolyn?

Pastor: I don't know. What do you think?

David: I guess I should. It's not fair for her to have to tag along with me. I don't know what I want—that money hangs over my head . . . I've been in colleges for three years now—and I don't know what to do. Carolyn should date other guys, but I don't want to give her up either. I can talk to her, and she understands.

The Answer. In this conversation, of which the above is only a small segment, there are easily half a dozen viable, moral questions about which the pastor should be providing guidance. Finally, David comes to an end after spinning out some of his indulgences and asks his pastor whether his conduct makes any difference. The pastor blithely says he doesn't know and turns the question, in a very unconscionable way, back onto David. There are some established values and criteria about ways one relates to parents, banks, college education, and dates. This pastor who feels no compulsion, whatsoever, to comment on any of these, fails to offer guidance and thereby deflects his pastoral authority and opportunity for moral care onto hapless David. The minister fails to address the moral issues that swirl about David and indulges in the immorality of avoiding constructive moral guidance.

Are there limits? Yes, there are. The pastor should have answered something like, "Carolyn is a symbol to you of the indulgences you manipulate from others." The missing technique is to guide David's attention and concern to the moral fireworks burning holes in his life. The pastor can be responsive to that moral responsibility without being moralistic or coercive.

Manipulated Debate
The Problem: A city church faces the alternative of going out of existence or of generating enough interest to sustain its ministry at its present location. One way of obtaining the latter objective is to construct a new building that would draw attention and perhaps people. In debating this issue, the

pastor sees a new building program as serving two desirable ends: (1) he will be known for his creative and constructive rescuing activities, and (2) more people will be drawn to the church and its life. The pastor wants his building program so he fills the church calendar with small group discussions designed to air the problem. The dialogue below follows such a discussion.

John: I really have some doubts about the way you handled the building program.

Pastor: *(Quickly, with some defensiveness)* Oh? What do you mean?

John: I'm just not sure that I would have advocated building, so strongly.

Pastor: I just gave them the facts. If the church doesn't build, it is going to die.

John: That may be true, but you were so directive that you didn't give the people much of a chance to decide what they wanted to do themselves.

Pastor: *(Very defensively)* You don't say! I organized the discussion groups so everyone could give an opinion on the matter.

The Answer: Cross-purposes at work again! The pastor has employed the technique of using small groups to process church agenda, but in this situation he establishes groups so that their conclusion will accord with his preconceived idea of what he wants. John challenges the pastor's technique. "Manipulated debate" suggests the exploitive nature of this pastor's care.

He controls the group and presses its conversation to his decision. However, the motivation needed to raise $125,000 in less than a year is a group concern that the process groups probably have not claimed. Thus, the pastor's technique of using group process to manipulate decisions leaves the congregation impotent, fragile, resentful, and ripe for rebellion.

John is right. Facts were withheld, crafty manipulation was at work, not pastoral care.

The answer is that the pastor be honest about the data processed by the group. Groups should not be used to guarantee or legitimize ends in accordance with the pastor's desires. One should come to trust others and their good judgment.

B. *Situational Uncertainty*

The second major problem area in pastoral care is well depicted by the image of drifting along. This image suggests the difficulties that are produced when the pastor depends on someone else for his or her relational and theological energy.

Running Scared

The Problem: A young pastor visits Jim, a seventy-one-year-old man who is in the hospital with an extended history of emphysema, a condition aggravated by his continuing rebellion in persistent smoking.

Jim: I want you to pray for me. I cannot quit smoking like the doctor says, and I know these damn cigarettes are going to kill me.

Pastor: Are you upset with the cigarettes or with your own willpower to overcome them?

Jim: It's me. I can't quit. I prayed about it, but I haven't heard from God. I thought maybe your prayer would help.

Pastor: Sometimes when we think God hasn't answered our prayers, we really mean that God has not taken our advice. Sometimes that makes us mad; you seem upset.

Jim: I am. I wonder if God wants me to get better. The doc has already said if I don't quit, I'm a dead man.

Pastor: Let me assure you that God hears your prayers and by his presence will give you strength. Still, much of it is up to you and your willful desires.

The Answer: Jim lays the question clearly before his pastor. The doctor predicts that if Jim doesn't stop smoking he will die sooner, not later. His pastor, also fearful of such consequences, is even more afraid to challenge Jim to stop. Instead, he avoids the issue by trying to reassure. Wouldn't it be better to agree with the doctor and say, "He's probably right"? At least this would guide Jim to look with seriousness at the prognosis of his death in light of his rebellious and cantankerous behavior.

Failing to pursue a line that gives open guidance, the pastor speaks of God and prayer, but only vaguely, not with certitude. The pastor, drifting along on a raft of theological reassurance, does not want to face the direct consequences of Jim's behavior and the futile, if not blasphemous, prayer that might be offered to smooth over all things. Why does the pastor avoid the question of imminent death aggravated by a conscious decision to act in a self-destructive way, including the desire for a fix-it-all prayer? The pastor is afraid to take the lead emotionally and theologically.

Too Much Patience

The Problem: A new, youthful pastor calls on a self-made, well-to-do bricklayer Shorty White, whose philosophy of life is that hard work will always reap positive results. A family battle occurs in which the father's desires for work success confront his son's philosophy of life and use of drugs. The pastor stands by helplessly.

Shorty: *(In a half-laughing and somewhat sarcastic tone)* Yeh, Charlie never has been able to keep a steady job. Why, I got him his last three jobs (physical labor types), and what has he done? . . . He's quit them all . . . without even so much as giving his boss a notice! Why, Jim (Jim is a carpenter and friend of the White's) took him on as a favor to me, and what does he do? He walks off the job! He's just lazy.

Henrietta: *(Interrupting in a somewhat submissive and persuasive tone)* Now Shorty, . . . (she then turns to the pastor and says), Charlie has always wanted to do something with his mind rather than with his hands.

Pastor: Oh . . . has he ever tried any work other than manual labor?

Shorty: *(Interjecting)* Yeh, . . . I remember when he got caught up in that Amway program last year and quit his job at the mill. He spent four months going to those fancy sales meetings, trying to sell their products and made less than $1,000. I am still paying for that one.

Pastor: You are?

   The Answer: The pastor is passing the time of day and offers no assistance or even interlude to the exchanges of

Shorty and Henrietta. The two responses that the pastor manages are indulgent and avoid confrontation. The pastor is either unable or afraid to move—rather than drift with the conversation—to make a comment or observation from a pastoral point of view. One feels that his pastoral patience will continue into an oblivion of ineffective ministry.

Had the pastor initially challenged Shorty or in some way affirmed the possibility of Charlie doing other kinds of work, he might have at least provoked Shorty's attention. Instead of patiently passing the time of day, the pastor should have confronted the overflowing and destructive negativity of Shorty. The needed challenge will be voiced only when the pastor is willing to forsake drifting and begin to care.

Grow Up

The Problem: This incident occurs in a senior high youth group. Sally, a freshman at a state university, had participated in the senior high youth group through the previous summer. Since attending college she has come home every weekend, and, although there is an established young adult group in the church, she continues to attend the senior-high activities. At the same time, she complains about difficulty in adjusting to school. The pastor comments that he "wanted to pass along an invitation from the young adult class."

Sally: I don't know if I want to leave the senior high class just now.

Pastor: I realize that you and Joan (the teacher) have a good relationship, and I don't want to steal you from her. But I am sure that before spring is over, you'll want to start thinking about moving up.

Sally: You mean I'll be too old?

Pastor: No, not just that. You'll be ready to go on to a higher class—more challenging.

The Answer: Sally questions her inappropriate behavior with regard to senior high activities and asks the pastor, "Do you think I am too old?" The pastor knows full well she is too old and ought to move up: otherwise, he would not have issued the invitation. Yet, when Sally, cognizant of the problem, looks the pastor straight in the eye and says, "Do you mean I'll be too old?" he backs down. In his response he denies his own conviction, the conviction of the young adult class, and Sally's inner awareness that she needs to grow up and move along. Why? Because he is afraid to give pastoral guidance to Sally. She wants guidance, she's ready for it, but he takes it away at the very time she and other persons and groups within the church want to affirm it. He should have said, "Yes, you are coming to that age," or "Yes, you are." There is no need to abandon the field when someone presses. By being honest he would have been faithful to Sally, the church, her claimed maturity, his responsibility to provide leadership. Both the pastor and Sally need to stop drifting and start showing the discipline needed to grow up.

Whose Prime Time?

The Problem: After several unsuccessful public efforts to encourage William to attend church, the pastor seizes on the idea of calling on him at home late enough in the evening so that farm chores and tasks cannot be used to deflect the pastor's intention. Approximately 9:30 in the evening, the pastor arrives at William's home and knocks on the door. Gaining entrance, he seats himself next to William, who is propped up in an easy-chair watching a network television program. William acknowledges the pastor's presence, but otherwise indicates that he is not going to concede good public entertainment for the intentions of the lowly, local pastor. He keeps on looking, and the pastor sits in mounting frustration.

Pastor: What are you so interested in on the TV? *(Spoken with a big smile)* Fill me in on the plot.

Lydia: William, turn that thing down a little. *(He gets up and turns it down just a little and sits back down, keeping his eyes on it.)*

Pastor: *(Aggravated at this rude behavior, he decides to be direct.)* Let's not talk now while this program is on so we can watch it without interruption. When it's over, then we can turn the set off and have some conversation. *(He begins watching the TV with interest, commenting on various actors so as to annoy all concerned.)*

After 10 minutes the pastor begins a discussion on the merits of TV watching, giving a minisermon as to how sometimes persons get into habits that are in themselves not destructive but may in the long run keep them from some things far more important to personal development. From here he proceeds with:

Pastor: William, do you watch TV on Sunday morning? *(Having previously moved his chair, he looks William directly in the eye.)*

William: Naw. Ain't much on then.

The Answer: The television is being used as a screen to avoid the pastor. Initially, the pastor is caught up in drifting along with prime-time TV, permitting someone else to set the agenda, the pace, and the emotional tone. Finally, the pastor cares enough to claim some prime time of his own. A better way would have been for the pastor to walk in, size up the situation, ask William—"Is it all right if I turn down the television set?"—and then proceed to turn it off and enter into pastoral conversation. The pastor should take the initiative to control the situation and move the conversation in a direction fruitful to his intended purposes. The pastor did not come simply to pass the time of night by bouncing along behind the TV commercials and mock human scenes of network prime time. There is a higher calling and a higher responsibility.

C. *Ego-Inhibition*
Of the three types of crises in pastoral care the final one may be seen in the parish situation where the minister's restricted ego is not up to the match. The pastor feels inhibited and fails to marshall sufficient ego strength to control the situation so that the necessary guidance can be accomplished. These illustrations follow.

Taken by Surprise
The Problem: A young pastor (28) visits the home of Beverly, an alcoholic member of the church in her late fifties. Although she voluntarily admitted herself to a state alcoholic rehabilitation center, she checked out shortly, claiming she had to go home to straighten out her marital problems. When the pastor made a visit the next afternoon, Ralph (her husband) was in bed asleep; and Beverly and her mother greeted his arrival. In the presence of her mother she referred to the pastor by her dog's name "Cluck." Then she came over and sat down on his lap. Not knowing what to say, the pastor pushed her off, and she returned to her seat, telling her mother, "See, Mother, he just won't let me sit on his lap."

Without commenting on that rather remarkable behavior, the pastor begins:

Pastor: Have you been able to handle your drinking problem since you came back from the alcoholic rehabilitation center?

Beverly: Yes, I've been doing fine. There's been no problem. But I just had to come home from there. I knew something was wrong, and you see it was. Ralph is taking a nap right now. He's been upset with me.

The Answer: It might come as a shock to most pastors to find a parishioner lodged on his or her lap. What is more remarkable than the initial phenomenon is that the pastor is so tongue-tied and ego-exasperated that there is a failure to comment on the incident or to use it to find out what is going on. The conversation begins as if the incident had never occurred. The pastor naively asks Beverly if she is handling her drinking problem. There is certainly another issue which she has not handled very well—her sexuality. If the pastor finds it impossible to comment on the sexuality expressed in Beverly's impulsive behavior, is he able to raise meaningful questions about Beverly's drinking problem? No, he is not. If the pastor is too inhibited to deal with the immediate situation, how well will he handle less immediate and more demanding experiences? The pastor and Beverly need to know what was going on between them when she came over and sat on his lap. He needs to address the question. It is scary, but it is necessary and ego strength is required.

Unnecessary Defensiveness

The Problem: A laywoman is working with the pastor trying to develop a children's evening program. The time mutally agreed upon had been changed, and arbitrarily so by the pastor. The woman is concerned about why this has occurred. She is very straightforward about the problem.

Joyce: *(Referring to her husband and herself)* We both have an immediate concern that we would like to discuss. We noticed in the newsletter, run off Thursday, that the time for the children's program was changed from the time set up. And we want to know why.

Pastor: I changed it.

Joyce: Pastor, this makes me a little mad. Did you not feel any responsibility to at least call me and let me know?

Pastor: No, I did not. *(With emphasis)* I am the minister of this church and I make the final decision.

The Answer: Joyce appears to have an important issue. An agenda and time were established mutually, but the pastor arbitrarily changes them to suit his own interests. He is honest in claiming that his reason is within his authority, but his response indicates personal insensitivity and a weak ego that seeks to strengthen itself at the expense of more healthy ones. The relationship between Joyce and her pastor does not evidence mature pastoral care. Instead of defending himself, the pastor should guide Joyce to some understanding of the reason the decision was made and move to secure his relationship with Joyce.

Pushing the Pastor Around

The Problem: A young pastor, recently assigned to a church, has accompanied a senior high group on an outing to a recreation center. One of the adult laypersons serving as chaperone has arranged for the youth group to use a miniature golf course for half price with the stipulation that all twenty-three members of the group participate. When the group arrives at the golf course, another adult requests that the pastor ask the group what they want to do; the pastor complies.

Pastor: Okay, if everyone goes, we can get in for half price.

Some of the group: Great! Let's go!

Leesa: I don't really want to play, but if you all want to, I will.

Lynn:	I don't want to play.
Geneen:	We'll just sit on the bus.
Pastor:	The group can't get the discount if everyone doesn't go.
Denise:	*(Sulking)* We still won't go.
Pastor:	*(Exasperated)* Well, do the rest of you want to pay the full price to play?
Others of the Group:	No. We can't afford it. We won't have enough money for the amusement park tomorrow night.
Pastor:	*(Angry)* Okay. If you are all sure, that means we'll just go back to our rooms for a while, then take our group for a walk on the beach, half-hour devotions, and call it a day.

The Answer: Earlier in the evening the plan should have been announced, including the intention and unquestionable expectation that the entire group would visit the golf course. By waiting until the last minute the pastor aggravated the girls, he invited their rebuff and their capacity—through their recalcitrance—to control the entire youth group. For the sake of argument, and for the enjoyment of pushing people with weak egos around (including pastors), Denise and her cohorts "control" twenty-three lives. The pastor should have announced the golfing activity with firm certainty, indicating that they had agreed upon it and that everyone needed to cooperate. But such is not the case, and another church effort to express care is headed for disaster.

Limits Need To Be Stated

The Problem: This situation involves a small church in which Johnny, a graduate student in religion, has been pinch-hitting in a Sunday school class during most of the year. It is late spring, and the student faces the long-hoped-for reality of his own graduation. It was initially agreed that he would have a replacement in two or three weeks, but as time wears on no replacements are in sight and graduation is around the corner.

Johnny: How 'bout the new teacher for the class—have you had any luck in finding one?

Lyle: No, it keeps slipping my mind. I've been so busy organizing the junior-highs and the church supper and all, and there aren't many candidates who are willing to teach senior-highs that the kids would go along with.

Johnny: Most of the people I can think of that would be good are parents of someone in the class, and that just wouldn't work out. I asked the class who they thought would be a good teacher, and they didn't much care . . . as long as it wasn't one of their parents and it was someone under thirty-five.

Lyle: I just can't think of anyone. . . . There is one man I just thought of. He's new in the community, and it might be good to get him more involved in the church. I'll check with him and see if he would be willing to teach. If not, I'll check with those other two you mentioned.

Johnny: I'd really appreciate it. It would be good to get someone by the time we start the next study series. By the way, do you know of any good curriculum for a New Testament survey?

The Answer: What Johnny fails to communicate, either directly or indirectly, is that he is not going to be there for the start of the next study series. Lyle really is not aware of this. Had Johnny been open and honest about the limits of his own personal schedule, Johnny and Lyle would have felt better about the situation. Johnny's ego simply is not up to the point of confronting Lyle with the reality that he will not be there much longer. Johnny should have said, "You know that my last Sunday here is May 30 and after that you'll be on your own. If there is any way I can help, I would like to. But after May 30 I will no longer be here. I hope you understand that." Johnny apparently lacks the ego strength, not only to set limits on Lyle's demands, but to state with some honesty the limits of his own commitment.

II.
Overcoming the Crisis

These are the problems! What can be done about them? This book is written to suggest some specific ways to overcome the problems of caring common to clergy and laity in local parish congregations. Most problems can be traced to simple transactional dynamics between human beings. These dynamics become destructive because the principals are unaware how they affect others and how others affect them. Good intentions don't have to end up as further crises.

We want to provide a practical, down-to-earth guide that will allow persons in the local congregation to minister effectively, with clarity and charity, and will develop in them the capacity to offer effective pastoral care. We hope to avert the experiences of ineffective and frustrated ministry illustrated in the case studies. There are ways Christians can serve and minister by providing guidance, establishing controls, and helping the outcome move in a theologically responsible direction. In presenting assertiveness as a new model for providing guidance in pastoral ministry, we hope to overcome the crisis in pastoral care.

CHAPTER 2

ASSERTIVENESS
THAT IS CARING

The crisis in pastoral care is dramatically evidenced in the local congregation. It proceeds partly from a deficient model of guidance as caring and partly from specific needs for guidance that have been neglected or misinterpreted. In the previous chapter we suggest that training in pastoral care for crisis ministries draws upon an effective model but one of limited usefulness. That model assumes healing and sustaining are the only appropriate modes of ministry and fashions professional perspective accordingly. This perspective does not affirm guidance, assertiveness, and control as legitimate or positive activities of pastoral care.

We challenge this perception at both the theoretical and practical levels and argue that pastoral assertiveness and guidance are essential dimensions of ministry. In chapter 1 we illustrated some problems incurred in local church ministry because pastoral assertiveness was not exercised. In this chapter we begin the constructive and innovative task of setting forth a model for pastoral care showing that assertiveness is caring. This model is based upon contemporary personality theory, upon the claim that competitiveness and assertiveness can be constructively employed in ministry in general, and upon the perception that parish ministry generally occurs in open or field situations that require resourceful assertiveness, if pastoral care is to be effective.

I.
Assertiveness Can Be Pastoral

Frequently, assertiveness is linked with efforts to control, to manipulate, and to exploit. One may conclude that a general attitude of assertiveness is a self-serving intention of pushing others around to gain unilateral control of the circumstances. Caring would not seem to have a place in this kind of activity, whether it is called assertiveness or something else. But assertiveness, like other human emotions and behaviors, has a dialectical quality that may be too quickly overlooked or dismissed by ministers and churches. Dialectical means having two polarities, or the presence of two apparent opposites in a single whole. Our claim is that, at its root, assertiveness has a quiet, passive, responsive, inviting, vulnerable dimension, as well as those components more popularly associated with it like directing and/or controlling. We believe there is substantial theoretical support, theologically and psychologically, for a dialectical understanding of assertiveness. Thus, there is a place for pastoral assertiveness in all functions of the church's ministry, from preaching to administration.

Robert W. White, a clinical research psychologist, has studied the ways that playful and exploratory behavior among lower animals and humans seems to have its own *raison d' être,* suggesting the existence of independent ego energies. Playful and exploratory activities are not compensatory for other frustrations or failures; playful behavior has its own integrity and is satisfying in and of itself. In the following series of excerpts from White's monograph on this phenomenon, one notes that play, manipulation, and exploration, along with what White calls effectance, are all generally associated with what we call assertiveness.

The kinds of behavior described in this chapter are motivated by energies independent of instinctual drives. . . . We conceive of them as energies that are inherent in the mental or ego apparatus. . . . They will operate in their own way, and this way is most plainly revealed in exploratory and manipulative behavior, which seems to perform the service of maintaining and expanding an effective interaction with the environment. . . . Effectance [places] emphasis on action and its consequences. . . . The dynamics of effectance are equally present and immediate. Playful exploration and manipulation take place because one feels inclined toward such behavior and finds it naturally satisfying.

It is clear that in some circumstances satisfaction is correlated with increases of arousal or tension.[1]

Taking into account not only stimulation and perception but also action, effort, and the production of effects, I shall call the accompanying experience a *feeling of efficacy*. It might be described as a feeling of doing something, of being active or effective, of having an influence on something. My thesis is that the feeling of efficacy is a primitive biological endowment as basic as the satisfactions that accompany feeding or sexual gratification, though not nearly as intense. . . . With exploratory behavior, where results cannot be anticipated, it seems a better guess to say that feelings of efficacy accompany the whole process of producing effects. The activity is satisfying in itself, not for specific consequences.[2]

The capacity to explore, manipulate, arouse, increase tension, assert, and create an effect upon the environment has basic psychological integrity. This capacity is not a distorted or neurotic effort to suppress sexual desire or destructive impulses. The whole process of producing effects and of creating feelings of accomplishment cannot be reduced to a more primitive origin. It is its own center of power and energy. It is its own core of feelings. Seen in this light, assertiveness is a companion activity with effectance; it is not a defensive function; it is a dialectical, ego-expressive action.

Assertiveness is the experience of exploring, manipulating, playing, controlling, and of competing with, against, and within an environment. If White is correct, and we believe that he is, feelings of efficacy that flow from effectance suggest that assertiveness is a creative aspect of exploration, tension, arousal, and constructive manipulation of the environment. Assertiveness may be seen as an opportunity for mutual growth: to explore, to be explored; to manipulate, to be manipulated; to create tension, to be in tension.

Thus, we claim that assertiveness is a fully dialectical activity incorporating elements of passivity and activity, of responsiveness and initiation, of respect and challenge, of sensitivity and strength. As such, we conclude that assertiveness is dialectical and holds promise as a desired quality in ministry.

II.
Ministers and Competitiveness

Resistance among clergy to accept assertiveness as caring can be traced more to general character traits than the training received in pastoral care and counseling. On psychological tests such as the Minnesota Multiphasic Inventory and the Theological Students' Inventory clergy generally display a personality profile that reveals a sensitive, warm, likeable person who is sincere, calm, and dependable. Clergy tend to be somewhat defensive and passive; they have a wide range of interests but reveal some difficulty in being socially aggressive and evidence a related problem in being able to acknowledge and express anger in open and constructive ways.

Such a profile suggests the presence of basic personality constructs that are uncertain about direct, overt, manipulative, and aggressive behavior and are highly ambivalent about competitiveness, expansiveness, and assertiveness in general.

Competitiveness is one dimension of assertiveness. Competing suggests that one is matching wits, skills, and strategies against another's abilities. Assertiveness suggests pushing simply to gain control. The personality profiles of clergy generally suggest that opportunities to be competitive and to match wits and pit skills are greeted with emotional conflict and ambivalence. This reluctance undercuts enjoyment and winning in open competition; it introduces a hesitancy that is a subtle invitation to lose.

Defeat in competitive activity, about which one feels ambivalent, will support a nondialectical or single-factor perspective on ministry. If one is not good at competitive and assertive activities, one develops strategies that support and enhance the strength one can and has affirmed. Typically, for clergy, these are the strengths of supporting and helping that do not openly thrust them into arenas of public competitiveness. "Better safe than sorry" is the adage that expresses this perspective.

As a footnote, the "peace" movement of the sixties and the "social withdrawal" movement of the seventies—being a general young adult phenomena of Western culture—have tended to balance the psychological conflicts associated with competitiveness by developing an anticompetitiveness value system. This dual influence on seminary students, pastors, and laypersons in general has received a great deal of positive reinforcement in theological and ethical language. Thus, some of the major components in the current crisis in pastoral care derive from fears about being aggressive.

World peace, economic exploitation, social oppression, and moralistic manipulation as political and systematic issues of national and international relations are issues that impinge upon the Christian community. Additionally, there is the developmental issue of the personality development of the individuals involved in these major social and political movements. Robert White's notion of competence and Erik Erikson's notion of the crisis of industry vs. inferiority suggest a significant developmental crisis in assertiveness at a relatively young age (years 6–12). Their findings suggest that either one develops the capacity to engage in social and environmental relationships in mutually satisfying ways or one begins to experience increased frustration and heightened ambivalence for competitiveness, assertiveness, and resourcefulness when occasions for these strengths present themselves.

Our concern is that pastors who are highly conflicted about their own constructive and liberating use of assertiveness will tend to avoid situations of open competition and assertion and will influence parishioners to relate to each other in similar fashion. The chief theoretical burden in this study is that ambivalence about being assertive can be resolved in constructive ways by devising strategies for ministry that develop the full dialectical potentiality of assertiveness. Our concern does not stem from academic debate about assertiveness. It intrudes upon us from the failures illustrated in chapter 1. At stake is the urgency of ministerial effectiveness, the psychological residue of developmental crises, and the integrity of pastoral care as a supportive and assertive ministry.

The research of personality theorists like Robert White, Erik Erikson, *et al.,* indicates that attitudes affirming noncompetitiveness and nonassertiveness are defensive and destructive in parish ministry whereas the development of the two-factor, dialectical quality of assertiveness provides a liberating contribution for all. In addition to the issue of personality development there are the social and political circumstances of the typical parish situation. The assertive dimension of pastoral care needs to be developed within the congregation and its witness or engagement in the community.

III.
Assertiveness That Is Effective

A. *Ego Strength*
Ego strength pertains to the individual's capacity to operate out of a personal center of power and identity in social and intrapsychic relations and conflicts. Being able to perceive that relationships are dialectical (having two component

elements that are related, organically and holistically, though they may not appear so) requires that one integrate the diversities into meaningful and dynamic relationships. The more complex and apparently divergent the two factors or polarities, the greater the ego strength required to achieve integration. Ultimately, ego-integrative abilities are a function of the individual's ego strength.

Assertiveness that is caring is one of those complex dialectical activities that requires highly developed ego-integrative capacities. In order to understand the dialectical nature of assertiveness, we must initially look beyond the traditional literature and empirical data used so well in developing the sustaining and healing dimensions of pastoral care. Those writings and data have been perceived more as resources for developing healing and sustaining ministry rather than assertive ministry because of their rather uniform focus on crisis circumstances.

To develop both a method and a model for assertiveness that is dialectical and caring, professional salesmanship offers data and experience. This suggestion may come as a shock to some who advocate confrontation and assertiveness as forms of therapeutic intervention principally in crises of bereavement, family conflict, and personal growth, but who do not endorse the use of assertiveness in a social setting. The ongoing life of the parish calls for pastoral care that is not oriented exclusively toward crisis psychotherapy. Such a need occurs in committee meetings, in training leaders, and in church finances. It requires the fully dialectical expression of caring that we call pastoral assertiveness. For these kinds of activities a form of confrontation and assertiveness is needed that has not been developed in pastoral psychotherapy and crisis intervention ministry. The dialectical qualities of crisis counseling have been explored,[3] but the dialectical qualities of assertiveness require examination. Basically, it is for this purpose that our study is prepared.

In considering the potential contribution of salesmanship as a method and model for pastoral assertiveness, we need to be aware of both psychological dangers and theological risks that lurk there. And we need to address the reticence of most pastoral care professionals to endorse in any guise what they perceive as manipulation and exploitation. We believe, however, that "selling" can contribute to our understanding of the dialectical nature of assertiveness. A very sophisticated body of theory about human nature, interpersonal transactions, and psychological needs constitutes a sales professional's model of assertiveness. Empirically, the goal for the salesperson is to close the deal, which means delivering a product or service and receiving compensation. Here, some may protest that needs are contrived and intentions manipulated, and that no genuine service is rendered. Likewise, the intention of gaining closure on the relationships, so that a yes or no decision can be affirmed, may appear as foreign to pastoral care. But we insist that this dialectical relationship or model is still more subtle and that much ego strength is needed: (1) to be intentional about one's own goals, (2) to be in control, especially of one's self, when others need guidance in order to make their decisions, (3) to be able to call for a yes or no decision, and (4) to be affirmative of the results of the relationship whatever the outcome. With this kind of ego strength in a relationship, we have a model for pastoral assertiveness. What we want in pastoral assertiveness is not crass manipulation or insensitive extroversion, but the disciplined capacity to engage in the dialectical dimensions of assertiveness. These dimensions are associated with White's notion of *feelings of efficacy:* exploring, playing, creating, manipulating, relationships in which the dynamics of moving forward and backing away, of initiating and inviting response, are much in evidence.

B. *Field Situation*

Assertiveness is an expression of pastoral care requiring a strong ego to integrate highly conflicting situations. There are additional conflicts in the parish setting (known as the field situation by secular society), in which pastors and laypersons minister. The local parish is a competitive marketplace where secular values and theological convictions force the church to be assertive in its corporate activities and in its individual witness. If the proclamation of the gospel and the ministry opportunities for the community through a particular congregation are to be effectual in any visible, concrete, and meaningful expression, a fully dialectical approach is needed.

Our point is that indifference manifested as passive aggressiveness, overt hostility, and resistance to the gospel can be challenged only through pastoral assertiveness. If pastoral care is used in the field situation it must draw upon assertiveness, otherwise, the local congregation will turn inward and eventually experience spiritual and psychological stagnation.

IV.
Assertiveness Can Be Caring

The drive to be assertive is part of who we are as human beings, and assertiveness is necessary if the local congregation is to live and proclaim the gospel among its constituent members and in the community. For the parish pastor and layperson the real question is, can there even be pastoral care without assertiveness? In the parish, the dialectics of caring range far beyond the single-factor models of caring in crisis intervention. Caring in the parish is dialectical (two functions, or dipolar) in the fullest sense of the word. In parish life, support and sustenance have to be related directly to guidance and assertiveness.

What is lacking in many congregations is an explicit understanding and overt commitment to pastoral assertiveness as a caring activity for both clergy and laity. We want to challenge this failure to perceive assertiveness as a positive activity theologically and psychologically. The rest of this book is devoted to developing a model for understanding and a method for employing pastoral assertiveness. The crisis that we observe in pastoral care has its principal locus in the parish because the parish situation calls for a fully dialectical or dipolar perspective on caring. Pastoral assertiveness is without question a dialectical or two-function activity. It provides a dipolar perspective on ministry and enables pastoral care to make a sustained, systematic contribution to all aspects of ministry.

CHAPTER 3

ASSERTIVENESS
THAT IS SELLING

Assertiveness, guiding, leading, directing, manipulating, and exploring are activities that arouse considerable theological and psychological fear and anxiety. The church's ministry is properly understood as a sustained effort to express the fullness of God's love to and in the world. A significant expression of God's relationship with the world is encompassed in the supporting and sustaining activities of the church. This is seen in its liturgy, in its study, and fellowship, and in its proclamation of selfless service to humanity in the name, and for the sake, of Jesus Christ. These are the genuinely positive and affirmative Christian activities moving against the destructive powers of military, political, economic, cultural, and religious values and actions that brutalize life and inflict suffering.

The church's witness in a world where evil principalities and powers are in ample evidence requires an assertiveness that is active and passive. One mode of assertiveness is the passive resistance in support of a cause as advocated by Thoreau, Gandhi, and King. That is one way to announce the gospel, the claims of Jesus Christ, and the church. Another type of assertiveness is active confrontation. This mode is oriented toward moving out—into—or even against the environment of the world. The Great Commission, "Go therefore and make disciples of all nations . . ." is a theological expression of this movement and in psychological terms, the same behavior is expressed in Robert White's concept of competence. "This way is most plainly revealed in exploratory and manipulative behavior, which seems to perform the service of maintaining and expanding an effective interaction with the environment."

The experience of going into the world to make a difference can be compared to selling. And since we maintain that assertiveness is dialectical, assertiveness that is pastoral is both caring and selling. The parish minister now has a new model for pastoral care that affirms and demonstrates the operational and theoretical integrity of confrontation and assertiveness, of caring and selling, in *both* personal *and* social relationships.

I.
Call for Assertiveness

In seeking to minister to the wounds of the world, the church claims a theological and psychological stance that opposes power plays, political coercion, war, and economic oppression. The paradox that suffering quietude is an effective opponent of evil forces reveals an underlying truth that is frequently driven underground. All forms of opposition are varieties of assertiveness, whether combative or passive resistance. Thus, activities of guiding, compelling, manipulating, and controlling are not, *a priori,* negative theological values or psychological motivations.

In fact, if we accept any of Robert White's thesis, God has given all human beings ego energies that are channeled specifically in the direction of effectance, control, power, and assertiveness. In short, there is satisfaction in asserting oneself, in being an effective manipulator of the environment—in fun and play as well as in serious theological and social struggles.

Thus, we maintain that human beings are endowed—both theologically and psychologically—with the capacity and the gift to control and to dominate. In Genesis 1–3, humanity is given dominion over all creation to engage in responsible control of higher and lower life. The capacity to assert and control is a gift belonging to human beings and their communities, including the church and its life in the world. Asserting and controlling are not sins or pathologies. They are gifts of grace and opportunities for growth. These truths are self-evident from the Scriptures, from the traditional missionary activities of the church, and from modern psychological understanding of basic human motivation.

Clergy generally have lost this vision both in training and in practice. Theoretical models need to be altered or replaced, and practical supervision needs to incorporate a wider theological dimension of human interaction with the persuasive activities of the God who creates. We hope to recapture this vision in ministry of the positive possibilities of asserting, directing, and controlling. Admittedly, danger lurks in such an adventure. The temptation to exploit and destroy others is ever present. The presence of such danger is no excuse, however, for failing to consider the constructive use of assertiveness to control, direct, and decide. As Christians we are called to proclaim, to minister, to direct the affairs of God's creation, and to be open to the new directions and creative activities that God offers us, his chosen people. There are risks that accompany the Christian's call to exercise dominion and to introduce novelty in this world. But God is with us in both, because God is both.

II.
Selling As a Model for Caring

What exactly are the theological and psychological dangers and risks in controlling and directing, in pressing for decisions, and calling for commitments? We will not know until these themes are examined in a setting that reveals their essential character. And we believe that setting is professional sales work.

A sophisticated theory about human nature, interpersonal transactions, and psychological needs and desires supports the sales representative in his or her work. These data are carefully refined and copiously researched. The goal in all sales work is to "close the deal," which means to deliver a product and to receive compensation that is the free and clear possession of the salesperson.

One may protest that such direct goals are primitive, immoral, and unethical or otherwise questionable as examples of crass manipulation or exploitation and certainly not related to pastoral care. Most pastors receive their pastoral care training in a theological setting where client-centered psychotherapy has been found helpful. Client-centered therapy as well as other forms of therapy and caring depend upon personal and contextual assertiveness that is—however subtle—a form of selling and manipulation. Pastoral counseling, at its best, employs the assertive dynamics of selling. Thus, selling as a model for caring is eminently worth exploration.[1] The perspectives, procedures, and dynamics of the selling model offer explicit concepts helpful to our understanding that pastoral assertiveness is caring and selling. Let's consider the selling model and its possible contributions to a new vision of pastoral care.

We argue that the selling model (in the present cultural and theological context of the church's ministry) provides a paradigm for understanding the dynamics of guiding, directing, calling for a decision, and affirming the benefits of what one chooses. These are tangible and observable behaviors. From the Christian perspective of parish ministry, we can approach the selling model and select those elements of selling that can serve in a theological context to enhance pastoral assertiveness. The limits are also clear: pastoral assertiveness must complement and enhance the claim of the gospel to redeem evil. Many will acknowledge that pastoral care and counseling draw readily upon explicit personality constructs from secular psychotherapy. Likewise, pastoral care may draw upon specific concepts in selling. Use of specific constructs from either sales or personality theory does not imply *a priori* adoption of a specific cosmology or economic system.[2]

If we are to develop guidance and assertiveness as valuable theological activities, we need to examine the best model available. We believe selling is the discipline that provides the best insight into the dynamics and significance of assertiveness. We suggest that the selling model has something positive to offer pastoral theology and that it does not defrock the clergy, corrupt theology, or undermine the ministry of pastoral care. Anxiety about the need to be assertive and inexperience in this mode are likely to be the sources of any unease with this venture.

III.
The Potential Contribution of Selling to Pastoral Care

Not all areas of sales work are germane to ministry, but several aspects of sales practice present needed contributions in the development of a model of pastoral assertiveness. These dimensions of selling are the foundation for developing sensitivity in guidance that is caring.

In undertaking any task, it is most important to claim one's intentionality. To claim an intentionality or to own a goal is to control that goal in a definitive way and some of the possible means of achieving it. If the church does not claim or control its goals, it cannot offer God joyful service that has any final sense of direction or purposeful response to the Holy Spirit. In establishing controls and defining limits, one finds freedom. Where there is no control, there is no freedom. Without controls, there is no freedom in ministry. The ultimate value in controlling goals is to gain freedom, not to exploit. Thus we will need to explore the hows and whys of intentionality and control in life and ministry.

PASTORAL ASSERTIVENESS

Furthermore, when one wants to share a valued reality, especially a controversial one such as the "scandal" of the resurrection of Jesus Christ, proclamation will evoke some resistance. Clergy need to know what constitutes an effective presentation or proclamation even though the response may be no. We offer the sales presentation as a paradigm for intentional guidance in general—preaching, Sunday school discussions, evangelism, counseling. We argue further that the good sales presentation operates from the same premise and with the same dynamics as the "flow" of the psychotherapeutic interview or counseling session (see chapter 7). We contend that the flow of disciplined, intentional interactions is universal in Western culture.

The need to claim and control one's goals and to make a disciplined presentation is the conceptual foundation for guidance. In this study only three of the tasks of the church will receive detailed attention in pastoral assertiveness that is selling: (1) leading church meetings in which specific administrative decisions and group commitments need to be made, (2) enlisting and developing persons or groups for specific leadership activities, such as teaching or recruiting, and (3) creating and securing financial and property commitments in the local church. We believe that these are the areas of most pressing need in pastoral leadership because they establish the intentionality of the gospel.

The reason for examining the potential contribution of selling in parish leadership is to accomplish the Great Commission. We believe that selling is a discipline affording a model of the dialectical dynamics of pastoral assertiveness, and that pastoral assertiveness has direct theological relevance for the church as it endeavors to embody the gospel of Jesus Christ.

CHAPTER 4

THE FIELD-CLOSURE MODEL

Assertiveness in parish ministry requires keen sensitivity to the context in which care and counseling are ministered. Traditionally, well-known theories in client-centered, psychoanalytic, gestalt, transactional analysis, and self-actualization therapy have formed the basis of pastoral care and counseling. All these models presume, *a priori,* that the therapeutic activity will occur in the confines of the therapist's *office* or some other designated therapy setting. These schools operate out of a medical or homeostasis model: the organism (person, group, or institution) seeks to restore or return to a constant state of equilibrium, or health. Thus, we title this the *office-health* model. It forms the basis of traditional pastoral care and counseling theory.

The arena of the local congregation and clergy is a different context. In this workaday world, pastoral care is not confined, theoretically or practically, to the office. Much of pastoral care is accomplished in a "field" setting where the measure of one's effectiveness is related to the interactional capacity to gain "closure" on values and behaviors in an environment that cannot be assumed therapeutic or supportive. We call the model for this environment the *field-closure* model. It forms the practical basis of pastoral assertiveness.

I.
A Proposal

We propose the field-closure model as a necessary and complementary companion to the office-health model. The chief difference between the two is context. Office surroundings effect the therapeutic setting in the office-health model, while personal assertiveness is needed to control the context in the field model. In both settings the dynamics, goals, and opportunities are the same, and the pastor may offer effective pastoral care in either setting.

The parish or field minister does not have therapeutic controls as readily available as the one whose context is typified by the office-health model. Personal assertiveness is essential in the field-closure model; personal control is the central dynamic where a therapeutic context is not a given.

Both models utilize assertiveness and control. Context provides control in the office-health model. Personal assertiveness or some field event controls the field-closure model. Ministers need to understand that controls are being exercised and received, and they need to be aware of how those controls are being expressed and experienced.

We believe that the need for pastoral care occurs in three major settings. The first is the crisis center where the pastor, because of spiritual gifts and professional skills, is asked to take charge. The second is the living room or "other" culture, where another person or circumstance controls the context. The third is what we call the circus tent to describe neutral political territory where control is available to those who assert their power.

II.
Closure in the Crisis Center

This setting includes the pastor's study, the counselor's office, the hospital emergency room, or the intensive care unit. The major variables are controlled by circumstances and the resident expert. The professional person operates with controls virtually guaranteed by the setting.

For example, a parishioner comes to the pastor's study for counseling. Without question that person enters the minister's territory. The study is the pastor's home base, and he or she tends to control due to circumstance and context.

If one goes to a hospital emergency room, one trespasses or enters the medical staff's territory and comes under their control. The pastor who visits the intensive care unit does not have to struggle much to communicate because both he and the patient know that the situation is critical. Prayer, or other resources pertaining to acute spiritual distress, can be readily used. The crisis center context or setting communicates urgency and necessity. The setting controls the situation for the pastor, so establishing ministerial rapport and providing helpful pastoral care is relatively easy.

The episodes and traumas that occur in emergency rooms, jails, intensive care units, counselors' offices, or pastors' studies are usually of short duration. In birth, death, pain, suffering, and divorce, the crisis is relatively short-term. The setting has been secured emotionally and politically for the professional. Context controls, or at least tips the balance, by favoring a professional who quickly becomes emotionally detached from the victim, patient, or parishioner after the crisis passes. The person coming for help senses that the professional is in control.

In the crisis setting, the need for help is critical and intense. But generally, neither the situation nor the professional's control will extend over a long period of time. Everyone anticipates that the injured person will soon return home, healthy and functioning normally. The critical incident is outside the immediate control of the parishioner, patient, or victim.

III.
Closure in the Living Room or "Other" Culture

The situation is reversed in the "other" culture. The professional may be a doctor, minister, law enforcement officer, parole warden, solicitor for charitable or ideological causes, or door-to-door salesperson.

Here, the professional recognizes that he or she does not control the situation. The living room or different cultural setting belongs to someone else; it is another's domain or territory. The individual in the living room or other culture is accustomed to calling the shots or making the decisions and exercises both conceptual and emotional control. The owner or inhabitant controls the context, the professional does not.

Whoever enters and for whatever purpose, the intruder stands initially on alien or foreign ground. In this setting the pastor explores, asserts, and controls circumstances only through personal power and interpersonal transactions. Far more ego, sensitivity, and understanding of goals to be achieved and decisions to be made are required here than in the crisis center setting. In the crisis center, context provides control for the pastor. In the living room or alien culture, the pastor's "person" has to create the control.

Frankly, many of the clergy avoid pastoral calling because they are unable either to control or grasp the dynamics that would allow them to be intentional about their visit. In order to protect weak, if not lazy, egos, activities of the local parish become increasingly institutionalized—that is, located in the church building. Some momentary gain in efficiency may be realized, but the psychodynamics suggest that the minister fears being controlled and rejected in someone else's life space or culture.

Churches needlessly and destructively institutionalize activities away from the living-room setting. Institutionalization allows pastors to retreat within the church's walls where control is provided by the context. This shift in control leaves the parishioner on the defensive.

In contrast, we believe that the pastor must take the initiative. It is his or her task to establish rapport and a sense of commonality—to provide understanding, appropriate help, clarification, respect, and opportunities for growth—whatever the context may be. This is especially true in the world most comfortable to the layperson: his or her personal living room or cultural setting. In many instances ministerial service can happen more significantly and quickly in the other's territory than in the pastor's office.

IV.
Closure in the Circus Tent

The circus tent, or neutral situation, is potentially both the most threatening and the most rewarding. The image suggests a cultural setting of heightened activity full of surprises because anything can happen under the "big top." The clergy has no professional or cultural advantage over anyone in the secular, circus-tent world of contemporary society where all people are peers professionally and ideologically. Among these people there is often no commitment and little interest in the church. Indeed, many circus-tent people are parishioners who claim no deep, abiding allegiance to the church.

Beyond the confines of the office and the accepting environment of actively engaged church members, the minister cannot rely on the setting to facilitate the relationship. On the other hand, in the secular mind-set the clergy is free of negative values and stereotypes that some ascribe to the church and its efforts to minister. The truly secular lifestyle of many uninvolved parishioners is not lived in theological guilt or shame, rather, life flows in considerable secular ease.

A minister dealing with ideological and interpersonal conflicts in this setting is truly on neutral territory. For example, during a chance meeting at a shopping center with a young adult couple who are nominal church members, the pastor offers, "Sue, Tom, you may not have heard about the weekend retreat scheduled for young adults on marriage enrichment. I thought you might like to share in this new opportunity." In the circus tent, the values of a church commitment and the secular values of a pluralistic culture clash head on. It is a battleground of values and controlling perspectives however congenial the external facade may appear.

Conclusion

Most ministers have been exposed only to the office-health perspective in their seminary and continuing education training. The field-closure model has not been introduced in any direct or meaningful way. Yet 80 percent of the parish minister's activities take place in field settings and require field closure.

The field-closure model is absolutely necessary as a working perspective if the bulk of parish responsibilities are to be carried out without an overload of guilt. The pastor needs to learn the basic principles and techniques of leading, asserting, exploring, and controlling—especially in living room and circus tent settings.

PART II

CHAPTER 5

INTENTIONALITY
AND CLOSURE
IN ASSERTIVENESS

For Christian service to occur, an opportunity for ministry has to be created. Some occasions for ministry are handed to the pastor. These are the crisis situations. Most opportunities, however, have to be developed. This is where control and assertiveness enter as potential resources and facilitators of theological service. When one speaks of seizing an opportunity, the psychological dynamic is that of controlling a situation so that constructive possibilities may bear fruit.

Assertiveness and control go together; pastoral assertiveness depends upon establishing control of a situation so that the intention of providing pastoral care may be accomplished. In this chapter we will look at the means and methods of pastoral assertiveness by introducing the theological and psychological dynamics needed to gain closure in the field.

A basic ministry of the church is to provide guidance in theology and doctrine, in morality and ethics, in proper study of the Scriptures, in reverent worship, and in refreshing recreation. Guidance, like assertiveness, may connote oppressive and coercive action to some. However, non-guidance is not the attractive opposite of coercion and oppression. Guidance and direction are required if the church is to live and grow.

The biblical injunction, "Train up a child in the way he should go, and when he is old he will not depart from it" (Proverbs 22:6), is but one reminder of the need to provide consistent guidance and to gain closure in child rearing and family relations. The violence and rage that surrounded youth demonstrations in the late 1960s are a poignant reminder of the consequences of nonguidance and non-direction in parent-child relations. Feelings of enraged powerlessness emerged because meaningful guidance and direction had not been given or internalized; among many youths only a limited capacity had been developed for assertion, control, and creative use of power. "Permissive training" was ineffective and efforts to gain closure and thereby exercise power ended with pathetic and violent acts of self-destructiveness.[1]

The issue is not the presence or absence of guidance and assertiveness but the quality of the intention to guide. Various motives will be revealed in the different modes of assertiveness employed to gain closure. Thus, pastoral assertiveness is not an end but a means to an end. Disciplined ministry is always responsible to and preeminently guided by Holy Scripture and by church practice and tradition.

The church cannot hope to be effective in its witness and service if disciplined guidance is denied because guidance and direction are the basic elements for a potentially effective ministry. Still, pastoral care will not occur unless assertiveness and closure are acknowledged as means of caring. Without assertiveness, even the best intention lies dormant, and the pastor is stymied if not defeated in attempting to meet real needs. Purpose has no resolution apart from assertiveness and closure.

I.
Intentionality and the Gospel

Control for the sake of control is psychologically destructive and theologically immoral. A pastor works to establish control in field or circus-tent situations because (1) he has a specific value, service, or product to present for evaluation, and (2) because effective pastoral care requires him to be in control. Without control in the field, a pastor will see the gospel crippled and his intention to serve thwarted.

Of course, we are assuming that the pastor has a valuable product (the Gospel and Lordship of Jesus Christ), that the claims and values of the gospel are to be made known, and that the Christian faith is to be proclaimed and presented without apology. These are initial and essential assumptions for ministry—that one has a gospel to proclaim and pastoral care to offer—and to carry out these activities intentionality and closure are necessary.

One may reject these suppositions or refuse to claim them, and may assert instead that all control is undesirable and destructive. However, we believe the church, and consequently its pastors and parishioners have a guiding function in the world; therefore, if ministry is to occur, intentionality is an essential dimension of pastoral care.

We contend that a blanket of sensitivity and support are often rationalized and legitimized in a weak and unintentional ministry. But it is time for the church and its pastors to act responsibly in the field as well as in the office. Industry, business, in fact all professions, quickly dismiss members of their organizations who are unable to exert control and achieve closure in their areas of responsibility. Should it be any different in the church?

One reason many ministers shy away from guidance in the field is their own uncertainty about who they are and about what they are to be, offer, and proclaim as clergy. Proclamation requires that one take a personal stand with confidence. An insecure and ambivalent pastor is certain to avoid situations that exert pressure on his identity, calling, and uncertain belief in the gospel. Guidance, a valued function of pastoral care, will escape those who bide their time in a perpetual and self-pitying identity crisis.

For example, one can attribute much of the success of

those pastors in the revivalist tradition to their ability to present their beliefs strongly, however right or wrong others might view those beliefs. Firm and confident faith in one's product makes a strong presentation. Without exception, an uncertain and embarrassed faith produces a weak presentation, and therefore closure and caring do not result.

Let us illustrate the value of intentionality in guiding. A satisfied buyer, when asked why he bought one piece of property over another, proudly responded, "He (the salesman) told me it was a good deal." The successful salesman had given a strong, confidence-producing presentation. He knew he had something to sell, and his personal belief was transmitted to the prospective buyer. The pastor, too, must know himself and his faith and must communicate confidence in both.

II.
Ministry to Real Needs

We believe there is a need for the gospel of Jesus Christ. One may recall the old story that a "super-salesman" can sell ice cubes to Eskimos. The salesman might be highly skilled, but only the foolish Eskimo would buy. If no real need exists in the mind of the buyer, closure does not occur and a sale will not take place. Selling is solving problems; *ministry is addressing real needs.*

Pastors have to operate more like salespersons when in the field. They must care for real needs. When faith and values are communicated, it is because the pastor is persistent and sensitive in locating the specific point of need and desire in the parishioner, the prospective church member, or the professional. By doing this he shows how his product—faith or values—will benefit the person he encounters.

People may perceive salespersons as hard-nosed, calloused, and insensitive hard-sell types. While this may be true of a minority, the best sales personnel are acutely sensitive to "the other." They move with a person to the point of decision.

A salesperson who "pitches" by memory is mechanical, insensitive, and deaf. He makes the prospect anxious and defensive. If a purchase is made, it happens as much to relieve anxiety, embarrassment, and vulnerability as it does to try a new product. This is harrassment; it is not control.

For a pastor's proclamation to be effective in the field, it must be tailored to the needs of the audience just as a sales talk is tailored by a salesperson to the needs of the prospect. The pastor must engage and sustain the parishioner in an active relationship as he searches out real needs. Once the needs that he can serve are located, the ministering pastor will point out the benefits of the gospel in meeting them.

People who do not respond to the church's message are not necessarily hardened of heart, rebellious to the gospel, or callous to truth. It is more probable that the church has not presented its ministry in a way that enables them to locate their needs and see the benefit of positive response. If the benefits are evident, people will buy. People are always buying. The only questions are What? and From whom?

Some pastors so fear personal rejection that they avoid venturing into field situations. These pastors fear they cannot control situations *and* present the gospel. They retreat into relationships that are labeled loving, supportive, and sustaining. But such relationships are not ministry; they are self-protective activities because these pastors fear failure and are afraid to risk an offer of ministry. These pastors dread the response, "I am not interested," saying in effect, "I am not going to buy from you." In this and other situations the minister needs to control pastoral conversation so that he can locate the real need and lift it up.

III.
Dynamics of Assertiveness and Closure

In the struggle to relate the gospel and meet the parishioner's real needs, the pastor's leadership style is all-important. If we can lay aside the prohibitions against the church's use of assertiveness—or selling in pastoral care—we can learn from the presentation strategies of other professions. The church that perceives itself as uniquely different from the rest of the world is elitist and destined to isolation, arrogance, and ridicule.

The Holy Spirit does not guarantee that Christian values or commitment are intrinsically more appealing than other value systems. So why do people respond to the gospel? Because they discover they need it, because they want to be Christians, and because someone somehow shared with them ways that the Christian life could meet real needs.

A pastor who wants to proclaim the gospel is ready to consider the dynamics of pastoral assertiveness when he has a gospel to share, knows the market of a particular parish and the needs of the people who may be attracted to his congregation.

The methods available to the pastor for gaining control in the field setting, or circus tent of secular society, fall under two broad categories: (1) the pastor's own internal attitudes and values, and (2) the pastor's external behavior and action.

A. *Internal Agenda for the Pastor*

Long before a pastor engages in the contextual task of witness and care, he needs to prepare himself internally. The internal frame of reference has serious and direct—either positive or negative—consequences upon external activities. Control begins with mental attitudes about one's self (i.e., self-control) and about the people with whom one is working (i.e., group sensitivity).

1. *Self-concept is critical in effective ministry.* People do not want to respond to someone who, for whatever reason, does not feel good about himself. A negative or ambivalent self-image is not to be trusted. As a rule people are only willing to respond openly to persons who exhibit self-esteem and thus seem trustworthy. The message, the pastor is trustworthy, cannot be separated from the medium, the pastor is

experienced as trustworthy. Experiencing another's trustworthiness enhances one's own trust-readiness.[2]

Self-concept exerts greater influence on another's responsiveness than do cultural stereotypes. The power of trustworthiness can always override stereotypes surrounding ministerial or congregational status. Once this nation laughed at the ambition of a peanut farmer, but Jimmy Carter knew who he was and that his judgment of himself was more valid than that of an uninformed and untrusting public. Consequently, he acted to influence public or cultural stereotypes and convinced the electorate to accept his own self-assessment. An expression of ignorance and ridicule, "Jimmy who?" became the gleeful slogan of a successful campaign.

"You are what you think you are." Thus, the Reverend Jesse Jackson rallied Chicago's Southside Blacks to chant, "I am somebody!" Maxwell Maltz, in his book *Psychocybernetics,* notes that a person's entire personality can be altered if his self-image can be changed, and Scripture comments, "As a man thinketh in his heart, so is he."

A positive self-concept is essential for psychological equilibrium. This truth is much more evident as one ventures into the parish or field setting where the environment may be openly hostile.

Resistance, conflict, rejection, and alienation are terms that accurately depict the field situation. Without a strong and positive self-image, the pastor will be crushed by indictments such as: "Oh, he is just the preacher. He doesn't know anything about the real world or competitive business"; or, "Why should we involve the pastor? This is a man's job"; or, "Why doesn't the Reverend pay more attention to preaching and praying and keep his nose out of migrant labor problems?" or, "Preachers only work at 11:00 o'clock on Sundays."

Professionals who are trained to work in a field setting learn to respond constructively to overwhelming rejection and resistance. For example, the door-to-door salesperson does not accept the public's stereotype that "door-to-door salesmen cannot be trusted." With inner strength, mental attitude, and assertive actions, the field professional rejects these judgments and stereotypes, turning them safely aside.

The dynamics are the same when a pastor ventures out on a church canvass or when he calls upon a new family. In the field, the pastor must deal with the subtleties of parishioners' moves for control and must be aware of their stereotypes, prejudices, and confusions, and yet remain self-assured and self-composed.

Further, the pastor must counterattack public prejudice and ambivalence to his claims of honesty, integrity, and worth, unless he would be instantly dismissed as a public nuisance. Under these circumstances he dare not fall into a supportive and sustaining mode. He must assert himself in the face of conflict to maintain his trustworthiness and to provide pastoral care that meets the real needs of the other.

In the office or therapy group, the setting or context protects the pastor, making personal trustworthiness, authority, and power appear less significant. But in the field there is no one to protect or guarantee that the pastor will not be turned aside. The insurance salesman, the door-to-door salesperson, and the land developer all know that only a small percentage of their presentations will be accepted. They learn to live with that psychological reality and situational fact. To have one's presentation declined or rejected is not necessarily an indictment of one's moral character or psychological stability.

Ministers cherish unrealistically high expectations. The average pastor feels that 98 percent of the parishioners ought to like and love both him and his efforts at ministry. He is not mentally prepared to deal with rejections and emotional abuse in the field. To be a pastor such a person needs to mature. Naive assumptions about others' readiness to give warm acceptance indicate a fragile and shallow self-concept. Clergy with these assumptions are unable, or at least not well equipped, to handle the accumulative pressure of day in and day out rejections in the parish, and especially in field settings.

Many of the clergy and laity want to assume that everyone should love and like the minister. It may be important "to feel loved," but what is the purpose or value of this relationship? Does this affection focused on the pastor so that he can "feel good," distract from his ministry to all? Often it does, quickly domesticating him or her on a short emotional leash. Professionally, being liked is only important as a means of creating a mutually accepting environment in which people can respond to the presentation. Often in subtle and not so subtle ways, members of the clergy end up being controlled and told, "Do what I want you to do or I won't like you." In the face of this personal vs. theological dilemma, they frequently shrink into passivity around the early morning campfires of warm acceptance, disowning their vocation and their ministry. The self-concept of a minister and his or her calling cannot collapse in the face of rejection and counter efforts to control.

2. *Attitudes about other people must be positive and healthy.* Persons are independent human beings; they are not subjects to be coerced or manipulated. They are free to choose a better way if they are persuaded it is better.

The pastor who demands that everyone believe in the Trinity because *he* believes in the Trinity is in trouble as a theologian and leader. He may use his pastoral authority to punish those who disagree with him; or he may attack others to bolster his own ego. Such defenses, erected to escape the anxiety involved in openness and encounter, are self-defeating for everyone. Parishioners are not intellectually inferior nor are they fooled when a paternalistic pastor attempts to run over honest objection and critical inquiry in an effort to control. That kind of control is neither Christian nor human. Parishioners are not the pawns of arbitrary power. How often do we hear the sound of religious zealots exclaiming over the number of souls they have led to Christ. These "souls" are perceived as a series of little gold stars rather than as children of God. "The other" is not to be used to fight off rejection and bolster one's sagging ego.

To illustrate, an example from the secular world may help. When a sales representative points out the benefits of a life insurance program he needs to be authentic. If the words are said only to make a sale, the prospect will sense the interpersonal dishonesty. The dollar signs in the salesman's eyes will carry a negative impact that transcends words, and a mutually trusting relationship will not be achieved.

Or, when a pastor calls on a new family in the community just because he wants to break the old attendance record, people sense a selfish motive. And because they feel used and disrespected they will resist.

Speaking, proclaiming, selling, and controlling are dialectical activities. They involve listening, hearing, being sold, and accepting control, too. This is the true nature of dialogue and the dialectic of mature pastoral care. In practice, as the pastor is making his presentation, the other person must be allowed time and opportunity to demonstrate why he does not want to buy—*the one being sold is invited to sell back.* For the pastor this means being willing to reverse roles and risk the security of his position by being open to another.

Salespeople are trained to obtain decisions—either a simple yes or a simple no. The objective is not to gain a yes from everyone. Rather, the salesperson is taught that there will always be a certain percentage of rejections along with the acceptances. Therefore, the goal is to determine what that percentage will be and then to relate to those inevitable rejections with maturity and respect.

If the salesman determines that he will receive one yes

for every ten presentations, he is free to become excited every time he receives a no. When he obtains a firm no, he quickly concludes the relationship by thanking the prospect kindly for the time and moves to the next presentation because that presentation may bring the yes for which he is looking.

Paradoxically, the negative experience helps the salesperson move closer to his goal and, therefore, he goes forth to obtain as many decisions as he can, whether they be positive or negative. He is not preoccupied with fears of rejection, and he does not slip into despondency because someone says no. The salesperson who is frightened by the word no, eventually, and probably sooner than later, meets with failure. Fear of negative response so paralyzes this person that the would-be seller ends up buying his or her own rejection and failure.

How many pastors avoid entire areas of responsibility because they fear a no? They interpret a negative reply as failure and reject themselves as human beings. Consequently, they remain in the office and wait for people to come to them. No risk there. They avoid going into the field where they might be rejected (as well as accepted). They sit uncomfortably in the midst of their passivity and fear, failing to minister adequately.

A clear yes or no response adds clarity to a relationship. Such a response is a positive asset to a relationship and a response to be sought by the pastor if growth and maturity are to occur in his or her pastoral responsibilities and relationships.

The daring few who venture beyond the church office or denominational meeting face a subtle temptation; although these pastors handle the no with some equanimity, they need to be on guard when the yes comes! It may seem like an oasis in the desert—refreshing waters in dry and thirsty land. Momentary success feels so good that the pastor wallows in the experience and fails to move ahead to new opportunities to minister. Such self-indulgent bathing is narcissistic and self-serving. It is a subtle form of exacting a hidden fee, this one psychological, from the person being ministered to.

B. *External Agenda for the Pastor*

A trusting relationship fosters the most effective person-to-person ministry. If the person feels the legitimacy of the pastor's concern for his best interests, he will be open to the pastor's message. Just how this trust develops in short-term relationships is hard to determine. Suffice it to say that people sense when trust exists and respond openly and usually favorably.

It follows that it is important to concentrate on making the other person "happy," if not for a long period of time, then at least for the duration of encounter. If a pastor is intentional about this, regardless of whether the person concurs with his thinking, the chances for closure are increased. People must be seen in different terms than conversions or church membership figures. Those concerns of the pastor will take care of themselves in due time. Meeting the pastor's "selfish" agenda occurs only after people are convinced that the pastor wants to see them satisfied even when they choose to reject his or her assertions. Self-restraint from coercive pressuring creates a climate of trust and fosters a quality of decision-making that has long-term integrity. The minister needs, always, to maintain the capacity to say to the other person, "This is *not* for you," or to raise the question, "What is for you?"

IV.
Crystallized Goals Are Essential for Closure

If the minister uses attitudes and thoughts that relate to, complement, and reinforce his goals, he is much more apt to achieve them. In contrast, the clergy member who harbors doubt and focuses on obstacles instead of achieving specific goals, usually collides with the obstacles and fails.

Those in the revivalist tradition utilize crystallized goals when they conduct periodic revivals, exhorting their congregations to a life of daily prayer and Bible study. They recognize the value of intentionality and closure: "What claims your mind, claims you." Through thoughts and attitudes our lives are the beneficiaries of mental discipline. Top marketing and sales firms along with national and regional church judicatory officials call for periodic sessions of evaluation and rejuvenation. On a yearly, quarterly, monthly, weekly, and sometimes daily basis goals and objectives are lifted up. Both the field representative and local church pastor need to know where they stand in relation to organizational and personal goals.

But too many clergy have goals that are only vaguely focused or in far away reality. The need is for crystallized goals. For example, if a salesperson's goal is to earn $100,000 in a year, such a goal is too abstract to handle on a working basis. Therefore the salesperson plans his goals in manageable units. He calculates that he must take in $8,333 this month or $2,083 this week. It is easier for him to think in terms of $2,000 units as the smaller or crystallized goal to which he will principally relate. With each passing week and goal, he sets them aside and moves on toward the next week and goal.

Crystallizing manageable goals is required and freeing for anyone, including the pastor. One dare not underestimate the power of one's mental framework; it permeates the entire person—it is the person. Therefore, one must be mindful of specific goals: to secure $130,000 in pledges for the church; to enroll 200 new members; to solicit $5,000 for a charitable campaign; to recruit five elementary-level Sunday school teachers.

One needs to establish goals and then create the structure necessary to accomplish them. Goals must be stated in explicit, measurable terms, i.e., becoming bishop, completing a new sanctuary next year, beginning a vacation church school.

Conclusion

If effective ministry is to be offered, the church and its servants need to develop skills in ministerial assertiveness. Foremost is the skill of gaining closure in mutually trusting relationships. The local congregation needs to be confident and secure in its ministry as it offers the gospel to its members and the public. Knowing the gospel—that faith "once and for all delivered to the saints"—is absolutely essential. Next comes the willingness to be bold and forthright in sharing the gospel in various forms of ministry. Ministry cannot be generalized; it has to be specific and manageable: a day camp, meals-on-wheels, a pantry for the poor, a revival, a new education wing.

Risking rejection in Christian ministry is for many the most difficult and important psychological and theological barrier to effective witness. Still one controls the no and the yes with a positive and affirming attitude toward the recipient and the situation. Today's rejection is an opportunity for tomorrow's yes. Failure to crystallize, and thereby gain control of one's goals and facilitate positive attitudes in ministry, will escalate rejection and destroy opportunities for service and witness.

This church is committed to creating occasions for ministry. This means gaining closure on acceptance and rejection as related aspects of ministry. In psychological terms this dialectic is expressed as, "Don't be afraid of rejection"; in theological terms it means, "Don't be afraid of the Cross." Pastoral assertiveness is claiming both the yes and the no in Christian experience.

CHAPTER 6

DYNAMICS OF
PARISH PASTORAL CARE

The dynamics of the pastor's work in the field setting are similar to the salesperson's experience when entering another's home or territory. The pastor needs to develop an intentional style for communicating his or her message, otherwise a confused and hostile response will be evoked. Some people will reject or say no to the pastor's message; that's to be expected. But collecting noes or rejections due to poorly presented messages is inexcusable.

In the previous chapter we argued that the minister needs to control the dynamics of the circumstances by thoroughly knowing the product or pastoral service, claiming manageable objectives, and being able to maintain a positive attitude throughout ministerial encounters, regardless of acceptance or rejection. Now we come to the presentation proper. Here, as in the general context of ministry, controlling presentation flow or the dynamics of leadership is essential. Again, pastoral assertiveness is caring and selling; it is a dialectical function, having both a passive and receptive side *and* an active and assertive side. A disciplined, systematic understanding of the factors involved in presentation or in leading relationships is necessary if parish ministry is to be effectual.

I.
Pre-Approach

A leader does not hurl himself into a helping relationship or ministry without prior preparation. Instead, he prepares for his approach by obtaining data pertinent to his understanding of the future relationship or situation. The pastor needs to research background history, apparent needs, special interests, likely values and goals, and current aspirations and prejudices. All of this knowledge will yield situational wisdom and confidence during any later encounters and efforts to minister.

This type of research does not produce immediate rewards, but it yields rich dividends in actual relationships. It helps one to understand why people feel and act as they do.

Does the parish minister know and understand the socio-economic influences at work in the community? Does he comprehend the forces that have brought about the prejudices and housing patterns? Does she have a sense for the ideology of the community and for who wields the power and for the source of that power base? Is he in touch with people's sensitivities and sorrows? Can she relate to people's oppressions and defeats?

Often this information can be gleaned from conversations with people themselves. In other instances it is more readily conveyed by a third party as the pastor asks questions, listens, and observes.

For example, before a salesman makes a presentation, he always tries to have basic biographical and sociological information in hand. When a referral is given, he secures as much of this background information as possible from those who give him the "lead." For the pastor, the best single source of referral is the body of persons already participating in the congregation. These people want their friends to join them in validating (or buying into) the wisdom of their decision.

When the pastor has been thorough and professional enough to search out his prospect's needs in advance, the potential recipient of ministry is impressed. That person, family, or group quickly realizes that even before the visit was made someone was working on their behalf.

What a difference it makes when the one who makes the call says, "Hi, Helen." The caller is no stranger, a potential friend has come for a visit. If the church representative has no knowledge of names or the actual situation, the stark awkwardness at the door confirms the worst—a stranger is seeking entry. Initially perceived as such, the pastor is apt to remain an alien stranger. But, if he shows familiarity with the family's names and refers to several friends, he confirms that he both knows and is known. He invites a less guarded, less defensive response. The way is cleared for respect and trust, and people usually respond to those they respect and trust.

No amount of charisma can replace information systematically collected ahead of time. When the pastor moves into town, is conversant with the issues, the people, and the problems, he becomes one with them. With good pre-approach information, the pastor saves valuable time for he quickly cuts through secondary background material to the realities that are of essential importance to him in his efforts to offer Christian ministry.

All this may sound simple and basic. It is anything but glamorous; yet pre-approach research allows the pastor to speak and act confident in his knowledge and readily confirmed perceptions. Still, this is an area willfully neglected and pushed aside by the insensitive and ineffective pastor.

II.
Approach

Apologies, timidity, ignorance, the intrusive stranger, all lead away from assertiveness and destroy the goals of ministry. Furthermore, these negative and defensive behaviors invite the other to advance upon the poor beleaguered pastor and tell him or her what to do next. The church representative loses respect and self-control, and the opportunity for ministry slips away almost without notice. The other becomes the active leader (by the pastor's defensive default), and determines the course and intention of the relationship. The timid pastor's goals are quickly dismissed and forgotten. If he or she leads with hesitancy, the pastor becomes a respondent at the emotional, theological, and social mercy of the other. Simply put, the minister's presence and power are destroyed.

Compare this approach to that of the professionally trained and successful door-to-door seller. He reflects his enthusiasm through every medium: eye contact, voice inflection, and body language. He strides to the door without hesitation. His confident knock signals, "I am here. Open the door. I have something important to show you."

The good salesperson assumes she will be invited in. Employing the words and the body language of a friend, she uses the person's name often, smiles, and reaches for the doorknob as she cordially says (not asks), "May I come in." At that very moment she wipes her feet, preparing to enter because she knows the door will be opened.

The approach above has the express purpose of gaining entry and control and of establishing the salesman's agenda as *the* agenda. Encouraging the other to establish the agenda is to invite him or her to control the whole flow of the relationship. When this is carried to the extreme, the clergy's agenda does not even surface and is lost. Furthermore, hostility develops interfering with good communication. When goals are not aired, they cannot be obtained.

The pastor, finding himself in the parishioner's home territory, must move with the boldness and assertion of the door-to-door salesman. Sales resistance is just as high for the minister as it is for the salesman. However, it may be expressed in more subtle terms. The pastor must assume control and move his agenda to the front and center stage of the relationship—"I've come to talk about your pledge to the church."

Confidence is central to a positive presentation. Part and parcel of this mind-set are confidence and enthusiasm communicated through calm self-assurance. Pastoral assertiveness is expressed in a confident boldness that quietly commands a hearing!

III.
Set-Up

The set-up is an intentional process to establish control in a specific situation. During this set-up process several things need to happen: (1) Rapport needs to be established; (2) distractions need to be eliminated; (3) attention and control needs to be secured from other potential decision-makers; and (4) goals must be laid out. Until all four of these objectives have been reached, the pastor should not proceed with the presentation. Failure to establish even one of these objectives frustrates one's ability to reach closure—or a decision—even before the formal presentation begins. In such a situation, it is to the best advantage of the church representative to end the experience and go elsewhere.

1. *Establishing rapport is critical.* People only open up with those they like and trust. One need not spend much time in establishing an atmosphere of trust. As soon as one senses good rapport it is time to move into the formal agenda. The temptation is to linger and enjoy the friendship. But because rapport was established with a specific end in mind, more than friendship is at stake in this situation.

2. *Distractions must be eliminated.* If distractions are not eliminated, the parishioner will use them, perhaps unwittingly, to frustrate the pastor's goals.

If Mr. Jones is in the middle of a painting project at the moment the pastor calls, decide on a time when Mr. Jones can and will give his total attention to the visit. If Mrs. Smith is watching her favorite TV sporting event, arrange a mutually convenient time to return. The church's work is worthy of undisturbed attention; consequently, its representatives deserve respect and undivided attention.

What if, instead of arranging to come back, the pastor suggests that now is the most convenient time? Too many times the pastor sits down and paternalistically watches the balance of a television program because he is afraid to assert his agenda. He rationalizes this, calling it establishing rapport; in reality, he is losing control.

Boldness and assertion are not out of character with ministry. Clergy must have as high a regard for themselves and their time as any other professional group. To hide behind a cloak called "nurture" is a retreat to passivity and fear. Furthermore, it discloses a lack of clear goals and the absence of self-respect.

The door-to-door salesperson moves toward the blaring TV and says, "May I turn this down a little?" Upon reaching the set, he clicks it off. He controls any children present or sends them outdoors so they will not interfere with his presentation. He positions his chair in front of the prospect because closeness enables him to maintain control. This works for the salesperson. It might as well work for the pastor.

How can a pastor possibly exert leadership when he lounges in an over-stuffed easy chair ten feet away from the parishioner? Whatever needs to be done to obtain control, the pastor had better do it, unless he is willing to pass the time of day and abandon his goals. It might mean rearranging the furniture. It might mean going into the kitchen for a lightweight, portable chair and placing it close to the people.

3. *Decision-makers need to be present.* A real estate salesperson is taught to observe carefully the person who takes the front car seat. It may be the wife; it may be the husband. Almost always it is the decision-maker.

Frequently the salesman completes an effective presentation to the husband, who is ready to buy, only to have the agreement vetoed by the wife. Why? Because she is an integral part of the decision process but was absent from the presentation. The wife did not experience the sales talk; she was not sold. She did not experience trust in the relationship, and she reacted accordingly.

Therefore, it is important to determine ahead of time, when only one spouse is present, whether that person can make the commitment. Put the question, "If you should decide that you want to act on what we're going to discuss, can you do so without involving anyone else?" If the answer is yes—proceed! If the person says that he or she has to consult the spouse—stop. Go find the spouse right then. Don't proceed, or time and energy will be wasted.

Pastor after pastor will win commitment from one spouse when both are involved, only to discover that the commitment proves weak. Expecting both the husband and wife to be home at a certain time, the pastor is dismayed when this is not the case. He asks, "Where is George tonight?" "Oh, he had a rescue squad meeting he had to go to," returns the wife. Is George uncommitted to church activities? Not necessarily, but someone did a poor job of setting up a situation calling for a commitment. So George was left out of the pastor's great presentation. Had he experienced it, as his wife did, things would have ended differently.

4. *Be clear and specific about goals.* House calls are made for a reason, and that reason needs to be stated with precision before the pastor leaves the premises. Hopefully, the minister's goals involve something more creative than meeting a self-imposed quota of twenty calls per week or visiting every member of the congregation at least once every six months! Why visit Mrs. Jones this week? For what purpose? Has a goal been set?

The effective salesman claims his identity at the beginning of the encounter. He does not apologize for his goal. For example, he clearly states that he is there to sell the prospect a piece of property. There is little doubt about his role or purpose. The sales personnel and prospects have a clearly defined relationship. *The pastor must claim his or her identity if relationships are to bear fruit.*

Gimmickry does not lead to affirmation. When a stranger knocks, sample case in hand, and declares, "I'm just taking a survey in the community. May I come in?" dishonesty undergirds the entire experience. Resistance and distrust pervade the air.

Successful door-to-door salesmen use pure and simple candor: "Hello Mr. Jones. My name is George. I'm a door-to-door salesman, and I've been showing your neighbors something I think you might enjoy. I'll only need five minutes. May I come in?" The nonverbal communication is equally open—the face is warm, the posture casual, loose, and relaxed. The prospect knows what is happening, he feels secure with the salesman's honesty and feeling secure, the prospect is willing to listen and be open.

When honesty does not underlie the encounter, difficulties arise. For example, Mr. Simpson has been critical recently of his pastor's sermons. He has voiced his feelings, knowing that the pastor will hear of them and react. Although the pastor has not been in the Simpson home for over a year, within one week after these criticisms are expressed the door bell rings. The pastor gains entrance and small talk ensues. The new church school program (in which Mr. Simpson is highly involved) is discussed at length. Finally a prayer is given and the visit ends, but no mention of the conflict has been made.

Obviously the pastor wants to deal with the problem—he has come to visit. Obviously Mr. Simpson wants to deal with it—he has made his feelings known. Yet, neither one takes the initiative to deal with the issue in a direct, assertive manner. Hence everyone's goals abort.

Ministers frequently lay aside their feelings and concerns believing they are protecting the parishioner. But, in fact, they are trying to protect themselves and their parishioners from their own feelings of anger. This pastor, no doubt, feels strongly about the merit and value of what he has been saying in his sermons. Does his visit help clarify his beliefs?[1]

Whatever the pastor's goals were in visiting, they are not clearly stated to Mr. Simpson and are not fulfilled as a result. From the encounter Mr. Simpson may conclude one of several things: (1) unbelievably the pastor hasn't heard the comments yet; (2) the pastor is sorry he's been doing poorly and has come to demonstrate goodwill; or (3) the pastor has heard the comments and is afraid to mention his feelings. The minister's visit perhaps is a show of strength, but without candor his true purpose remains unknown.

Both John F. Kennedy and Richard Nixon wanted to be president in 1960. They said so. They both worked hard and argued convincingly for election. Open and direct campaigning is much less visible in the church. Hard work and effort in church campaigning are around all right, but openness and directness are missing. The Reverend Mr. Black wants to be a denominational leader, and he campaigns for that position. He is seen at the right places, says the right things, and meets the right people just like any other politician. But part of his strategy, long honored in church circles, is public disavowal of his aspiration to one day become that chief executive or pastoral leader for the denomination.

Traditionally this has been an effective political strategy because clergy are indoctrinated to be humble, meek, and unaspiring. Would that more seminarians could say, "I want to become bishop or stated clerk or president in order to use that office to implement my ideas for and about the church." Why? "Because I have confidence in me, my God, and the convictions of my faith."

Before attempting another home visit, another sermon, another book, or another meeting the pastor should ask himself—why? If he knows why, he can move with haste to that objective. If he can't say why, perhaps he should cancel all plans.

IV.
Presentation

There is no substitute for product knowledge. But ministers cannot and should not claim to be experts about everything in the field of religion and church life. When asked by a parishioner about the meaning of a passage in Revelation, the pastor replied, "I just don't know. I've not studied Revelation much, and much of what I read in that book confuses me." This pastor has done an excellent job of staying in touch with her own integrity. The parishioner is comforted by this disclosure—"I can admit there are things I don't know without being embarrassed." Dishonesty about one's knowledge feeds self-doubt. People detect fear and uncertainty and draw back.

Companies place their sales personnel in extended training programs where they memorize a "canned" sales talk verbatim and use it over and over again with great effectiveness.

A canned presentation may seem less than glorious to the uninitiated, but it has all of the logical processes of decision-making built in. Put together piece by piece, the whole is highly persuasive. With constant use, the presentation loses its rigidity and becomes part and parcel of the individual personality that uses it.

Why not the same for the church? Certain functional presentations such as recruiting and fund raising recur in the course of ministry. Have presentations been prepared for them?

If presentations are not ingrained, the uncertainty of the speaker is evident. A sermon may have solid substance and yet not communicate very well. Without thorough preparation, the best message sounds shaky, disorganized, and unauthentic.

Inflexibility, however, is not a characteristic of the well-rehearsed presentation. While speaking one should listen at all times. If the desired response surfaces, one should stop, call for a decision, and bring the interview to an immediate close, even though the presentation has hardly begun.

A young college student was thoroughly trained to sell Webster's dictionaries, and he had a presentation that noted *all* the dictionary's benefits. After several presentations and a few successes, he came to one prospect who, upon hearing what he was selling, said, "I've been meaning to get a dictionary for six months. I'll take one." The student was totally bewildered. Out of habit he started at the beginning of his sales talk and went all the way through it while the buyer patiently waited for him to finish.

The student forgot the ABC's of selling—*always be closing!* He should have asked for the order immediately instead of wasting valuable time. He was not being paid to make presentations. He was being paid to get orders on dictionaries—to close the deals.

A certain company automatically fires the salesperson who is at the bottom, two quarters in succession. This is a severe means of forcing an individual to compete and to improve. The church would only profit likewise by saying to certain ministers, "You are not making it. You would be happier and more fulfilled in another field. Both you and the church would realize greater benefits if you operated as a layperson."

The church has no direct accounting process whereby the pastor and his or her supervisor know the score. Attendance figures and a balanced budget are not conclusive indicators of a pastor's success. How does one determine if a sermon produced a commitment? How does one know if a home visit reached its desired goal? We believe the church needs to develop a system of accountability and responsibility for ministerial performance. Later, we indicate the shape of such a system.

V.
Trial Closures

In the sales process, a trial closure determines where the prospect is in relationship to one's final goal. By testing the mind-set of the buyer, one can measure the relative success or failure of the presentation. At some point during his or her presentation, the salesman will ask, "Do you see how this will be helpful to you, Mr. Dunbar?" If Mr. Dunbar's reply is a flat no, the salesman has to decide whether to continue or move on to a more fruitful encounter.

If Mr. Dunbar has no positive response after adequate presentation, additional conversation probably won't change his position. He has heard the benefits of the offer, and he has chosen to respond negatively. The salesman's goal has been reached. Mr. Dunbar has made a decision.

A trial close calls for the other person to indicate a preference, to make a commitment, or to point out a direction. Following a trial close, three options exist: (1) move to a new prospect; (2) give more information; or (3) close the deal.

If the parishioner is unresponsive to one's ideas, it is better to leave and not become overbearing. But remember, leave as a friend by thanking the parishioner for his or her time.

If the parishioner demonstrates interest but is unwilling to make a commitment, he or she probably needs more information. Take up the point of interest or confusion, return to the presentation flow, and again call for the desired commitment.

If the parishioner is pleased and enthusiastic, close the deal. Secure a commitment then and there.

Trial closure remarks should be a working part of a pastor's vocabulary for each type of presentation he makes. The following are representative of closure questions:

(1) "Would you get involved in the education program if this type of opportunity were made available?"

(2) "Does singing in the church choir sound like something you would enjoy?"

(3) "This would certainly be beneficial to your entire family, wouldn't it?"

(4) "Would you use this service if we could provide it?"

(5) "Does this sound like a worthwhile use of these funds?"

(6) "The more we put into anything, the more we get out of it. Isn't that true?"

(7) "Teaching Christian values is one of the most important things a parent can do, don't you agree?"

VI.
Closing

A. *Ask for a decision.* Fear keeps the pastor from calling and asking for a decision or attempting closure. To ask for any type of commitment is to run the risk of a negative reply. Anxiety about that possibility leads one to develop avoidance mechanisms to prevent the no experience.

One way to avoid that experience is to remain in the office, protected by a desk. It is possible to flee the field of another's territory, but few commitments or meaningful decisions about the everyday realities of a lively faith are made in the pastor's study. A church group may have great faith, but its light will remain under the bushel if it is not taken to the people who can then be asked to make a decision about their relationship to the gospel and the ministries it affords.

Besides, if the pastor never asks for anything, he or she will never be turned down. The world is full of this type of clergy. This man or woman goes around being helpful in theologically and culturally safe ways, hoping that he or she will not be bold enough to deserve public rejection.

PASTORAL ASSERTIVENESS

One has to be skeptical about this type of moral influence approach to ministry. This helping approach to ministry raises theological questions about the pastor's motives, and without assertiveness, it can scarcely qualify as pastoral care. There is a real need for pastors who will look directly into another's eyes and call for a yes or no decision. At some point the parishioner must have the experience of claiming or rejecting the church's values. An effective pastor calls for decisions and commitments.

Here is a secular case in point. A midwestern town has two laundry and dry cleaning establishments. Recently, when Firm A came under new management, the newest and best equipment was installed, employees were added to speed service, and the old building was remodeled. The entire operation was efficiently restructured—Firm A offered the most modern laundry service in town.

Firm B had been operating for some time; it had old equipment, a poor location, and the cleaning was not always the best. Yet, after twelve months of severe competition, Firm B controlled 75 percent of the trade. This seems strange until the one big difference is disclosed. Firm B *employed a fifty-eight-year-old man to go around asking people for their business. He picked up their cleaning and delivered it,* several days later. Firm B was willing to ask for the order to close the deal.

This failure at the vital nerve is not unlike many sermons preached on weighty issues of the day. With exceeding eloquence the pastor leads the parishioner step by step through the sermon outline. Yet, when the time for the benediction arrives, and then passes, the sermon is still drifting on the mists of dangling exposition because the people are not told what to do.

The preacher can give a provocative and moving sermon, but if a decision is not called for, he has stymied his own intense desire that the sermon strike home. *People have to know with clarity what is expected of them before they can respond.*

B. *Dealing with Objections.* People want to own a faith. But they also want to know that they are committing themselves to the right faith. To determine this they utilize objections as a means of clarifying their own faith decisions. Objections are a part of the commitment process, not an enemy of it.

1. *Ignore early objections.* Being the focal point of a person's objections produces anxiety that may induce panic in the unsophisticated minister. Many times objections are simply "pauses" in the other person's mind. The pastor who understands this about his parishioners does not misinterpret an objection as full-fledged opposition.

The assertive pastor responds, "Yes, Mr. Jones, I know just what you mean," and continues the presentation unmolested by a surface or anxiety-stage objection. If the concern fails to resurface, it is not a real objection! Little is gained by nursing free-floating, random objections into a serious and negative reaction. Allow people to stretch their minds and verbalize their mental energies.

2. *Deal with an objection honestly, however, if it continues to reappear.* The reoccurrence of an objection indicates that it is real and valid. At this point, the pastor needs to stop whatever he is doing, clarify and affirm the objection, and then deal with it openly. If it cannot be mutually overcome, the parishioner has reached a point of decision.

Possible objections should be anticipated and legitimate solutions, if they exist, should be thought out. If the pastor has a solution, he should propose it, return to his presentation, and move toward the final commitment or decision point.

C. *Mutuality: Doers and Others or Sellers and Buyers.* In pastoral conversation, someone always sells and someone always buys. The crucial question is, Who is the buyer? Does the pastor or layperson realize this subtle dialectic in the dynamics of all relationships? This is an important awareness whether the goal is to obtain a pledge, recruit a new Sunday school worker, or interest a new family in going to church. The prospective member, teacher, or donor is quite capable of making his or her objections so attractive that the naïve pastor decides to buy or accept a surface or contrived objection as real. In all human interactions someone is selling and someone is buying; one is the doer, one is the other.[2] The pastor had better know who is buying and who is selling.

Conclusion

For the local congregation and for pastors who struggle in their everyday efforts to minister, there are approaches available to facilitate the intentional enhancement of a strong and genuine mutuality. Unfortunately these techniques have not been appropriated for general pastoral use. Selling, in using the presentation flow, is a disciplined effort to enhance mutuality so that decisions can be made in an environment of mutual integrity. We believe the dynamics of pastoral care are those of selling, especially pastoral care that is appropriately assertive. The model of pastoral care that we advocate is designed to aid the pastor in developing pastoral assertiveness that is caring and selling.

CHAPTER 7

INTENTIONAL GUIDANCE IS PASTORAL CARE

Pastoral assertiveness establishes the value of maintaining leadership in circumstances where surface objections and resistance may be misinterpreted as real objections. The presentation flow is a means of moving toward desired goals. Throughout this study, the contention is that models employed by therapists and salesmen use similar dynamics and premises about human nature, change, and opportunities for growth.[1] Any apparent differences are in degree, not kind.

A self-conscious effort to strengthen the other and enhance mutuality endeavors to care *and* to sell. Many ministers who have received training in pastoral care and counseling (or pastoral psychotherapy) may deny such a kinship. Debating the nature of that kinship evokes a stimulating theoretical discussion of the components that contribute to caring and asserting. Our interests include, but extend beyond, theoretical debate. Our concern is that pastoral care draw upon one of its richest resources for ministry—assertiveness that is caring. Some may perceive psychotherapy and sales presentation flow as unrelated experiences, but they are not unrelated opposites. They are related, borrowing from the insights of Erik Erikson, as "dialectically progressive" forms of directivity.[2]

Our argument is threefold. (1) Therapy and presentation

are both instances of interpersonal relations[3] in which new goals are negotiated and the dialectical ways of approaching these new possibilities are dynamically identical. (2) Therapists, pastors, and salespersons all seek to create relationships in which the other individual or group (large and small) will respond in attitudes (feelings and feeling tones) and behaviors (actions, verbal and nonverbal) that are specific and within manageable boundaries. Such relationships present actual possibilities for enhancing the mutuality and strength of both the doer and the other. (3) The dynamics and dialectical intentions of good therapy and good presentation are similar. Both are forms of assertiveness essential to the pastor in exercising effective pastoral care.

I.
Self-Interest Is Needed for Mutuality

Selfless service cannot be claimed in ministry, counseling, or revolution against social oppression because selfless service does not exist. Any human activity requires an interaction of attitude and behavior of persons and/or groups; this movement is from a focused center and establishes the potentiality of a constructive relationship. In a constructive relationship, the ego or identity needs of both parties are affirmed *and* publically acknowledged.

When the client comes to the counselor for help or the pastor calls on the parishioner, the needs of the client or parishioner appear obvious. In such a relationship what are the ego needs or self-interests of the counselor? To believe that the needs of the counselor or minister are located solely in their desire to help the client identify and meet his or her real needs is only partially true. There are other self-interests being served more subtle than the obvious ones of pay, professional prestige, security, and moral victory. The interests of all are best served if the helper or doer (clergy, therapist, sales representative) is able to establish mutuality, rapport, or acceptance in the relationship so that he or she can meet the real needs of the other. This is done (1) by helping the other identify his or her own needs and (2) by being in control of one's own needs (conceptually and emotionally).

"It is impossible for a therapist *not* to act in terms of his own needs."[4] This statement by Carl Rogers expresses a basic premise of the assertiveness model. The therapist—as a human being—has certain needs that are being satisfied in the caring and selling relationship that are not necessarily "a distorted form of sublimation."[5] In pastoral assertiveness we assume that the pastor will take charge of technical details but will claim his own self-interests in matters of therapy.

Carl Rogers *et al.* remind us that the first step in developing a therapeutic relationship is the professional's acknowledgment that self-interests are central in all human interaction. Beyond claiming that general needs exist, a second step in therapy is to engage those needs in constructive activity. But, one does not take charge of or control therapy by trying to withhold one's needs from entering the relationship. Rather, control is established as therapists and pastors are open and free to express their needs and feelings in relationship. When a pastor endeavors to control without admitting his own needs because he fears he may lose control of his own theological ambiguities and feelings, mutuality, rapport, and trust are not established. Unless rapport and trust can be developed, the relationship will be out of control, quickly becoming mutually destructive, as it bounces about on a sea of mutual suspicion regarding whose needs and what kinds of needs are being met.

The client will move toward trust and rapport as he discovers that the therapist is meeting her own deeper needs. Is the therapist emotionally and intellectually secure, *and* is she willing and publicly able to have her unmet needs challenged and engaged by the client? If the client experiences the therapist as negative in either of these aspects, he will tend to pull back and protect himself. Why?—the therapist has over-controlled—she is unwilling to give something of herself to the client. Only when the therapist can give something to meet the client's deep and simple need for acceptance, will he extend acceptance to the therapist, thereby meeting needs in her self-interest.[6]

In summary, the client initially engages the therapist for help; the therapist is supposed to be in charge. Controlling the situation to meet the needs of the client involves freedom and risk for the therapist. The client can meet the therapist's real needs (self-interests), the simplest of these being emotional acceptance. But if the therapist tries to deny that she brings her own real needs into the relationship, the client experiences that struggle as over self-control or denial of self-interest and will not trust the relationship.

For the sales representative the self-interest is logging a sale; for the therapist it is achieving mutual acceptance; for the minister it is to affirm that we are all children of God growing in grace. None of these possibilities occur if the self-interests (real needs) of the person in charge are not claimed and expressed in open and courageous ways, whether subtly or directly in the relationship.

Just being in charge meets a need of self-interest. Therefore the issue is whether the pastor, salesman, or therapist is in control so as to facilitate a mutual meeting of self-interests. If so, a creative relationship is being established; if not, a destructive relationship is brewing.

II.
Pre-Approach

Good counseling, like good selling, requires preparation. The counselor obtains data about a client from many sources. The client may be referred directly by a professional colleague, family member, or friend. In such instances, referral is a positive gesture indicating that the counselor has the training, personality, and reputation for making successful "closings" in counseling. The attorney, physician, or family member, who has been impressed by these strengths, provides background data, directly and indirectly, about history, values, interests, goals, aspirations, and difficulties of the client in meeting his real needs. As a counselor, the pastor claims she will initiate a mutually satisfying relationship that will meet the deep needs of the client. She will offer him a mutually strengthening experience commonly known as a psychotherapeutic relationship.

From case records, medical history, initial intake interviews and psychological testing procedures the therapist quickly obtains information and develops an approach even before establishing the therapeutic relationship. Without data gathered from third-party referrals and personal research, efforts to establish rapport would be extended, frustrating, and often result in premature termination, that is, a negative closure.

Nothing can make a stranger feel more welcome than a friend. An informal, sensitive openness in the initial stage of the relationship invites a less guarded and less defensive response.

Finally, a reminder that the therapist is also prepared conceptionally and emotionally to engage in conflicted relationships. The counselor has had specialized training in concepts that direct the therapy flow and has experienced therapy as a client herself. Thus the pre-approach may have extended over many years of preparation. The therapist, like the pastor and sales representative, obtains data and training in order to establish control and construct a favorable psychological climate.

III.
Approach

A positive and open attitude that expects to gain rapport allows the therapist or salesperson to be sensitive to the setting (emotional, social, intellectual) and to establish the subject matter essential to his or her goals.

Howard Clinebell, in a discussion on the goals of

short-term counseling (formal and informal), claims that the two most important goals are to "provide a supportive, empathetic relationship," and to "help restore functioning by reducing the pressure of pent-up, blocking feelings through emotional catharsis."[7] The therapist assumes leadership by providing a supportive relationship which allows surface feelings to be released. This therapeutic release requires reassuring guidance and gentle control but control nonetheless. Unless the therapist, salesman, or pastor assumes control to support the initial release of emotional needs, he or she is held captive by personal timidity and reduced to a passive respondent, while control is handed over to the client. The therapist has to assume control of the setting, inviting the client to express his or her needs in an environment that is positive *and* controlled to ensure acceptance.

After this initial phase, the therapist begins to identify the agenda or needs that should occupy front and center stage. The transition from controlling the setting to controlling the agenda might be expressed, "We need to talk about your marriage."

Essentially, the approach in therapy follows the presentation flow in sales. The salesman or therapist creates a psychological setting so that the issues that the therapist has identified as significant for the relationship will be mutually joined. The dynamics of therapy are illustrated with insight by Erikson. He declares,

Thus the "doer" and "the other" are partners in one deed. Seen in the light of human development, this means that the doer is activated in whatever strength is *appropriate to his age, stage, and condition,* even as he activates in the other the strength appropriate to *his* age, stage, and condition. Understood this way, the Rule would say that it is best to do to another what will strengthen you even as it will strengthen him—that is, what will develop his best potentials even as it develops your own.[8]

In short, the professional (therapist, clergy, etc.) is expected to take initiative to create a setting and a relationship that facilitate readiness for a heightened mutuality. Honesty and encounter go hand in hand.

IV.
Set-Up

Rapport is essential for the relationship to move toward mutuality while the focus of attention is on obtainable goals. Setting the stage, Carl Rogers says,

I would like my feelings with him to be as clear and transparent as possible, so that they are a discernable reality for him, to which he can return again and again. . . . What I am and what I feel are good enough to be a basis for therapy, if I can transparently be what I am and what I feel in relationship to him.[9]

"What I am and what I feel are good enough. . . ." Perhaps. The therapist needs to identify and claim his agenda so that mutual intentions and goals can be "as clear and transparent as possible." Where the context provides control the "what I am and what I feel" issue may be satisfactorily answered indirectly. But in the field—in the other's living room or in a different cultural setting—the what-I-am-about question needs to be claimed openly and boldly: "I am Reverend Jenner from Immanuel Church and I'm visiting new neighbors in the community." This initiative claims identity and helps to establish rapport. Empathy and rapport provide the support necessary for therapeutic interaction. They are not goals in themselves; they are used to give strength to the individuals in the relationship—to enhance the mutuality between therapist and client.

After rapport is established, one moves on to formal agenda. Ministers who draw on the pastoral assertiveness model will not satisfy themselves with pastoral contacts that are limited in purpose and scope to "friendly visits to establish rapport." The pastor, like the therapist, needs to claim his or her identity if relationships are to have more than superficial meaning.

Three additional factors need to be considered during the set-up of the therapeutic flow:

(1) *Goals for the session need to be laid out.* Clinebell states, "If a person comes with a specific decision or interpersonal conflict, help him deal directly and responsibly with this."[10] Here the therapist controls and engages in intentional guidance by clarifying decisions or conflicted relationships so they can be addressed in manageable form during the session.

(2) *Tap the client's interests and resources.* Again from Clinebell, note the flow: "Mobilize the person's latent resources for coping. Help him discover and learn to use them."[11] The therapist helps to focus or channel energy and possibilities to help the other party discover his own power to control and create. This will not occur if the therapist attempts to do the work or provides her own resources. A mutual agenda helps the client discover his own resources with the help of what the therapist offers.

(3) *Eliminate distractions.* Only when the therapist is certain of his or her own identity, intentions, and goals can some interactions be discerned as distractions; otherwise, any tidbit of experience may appear relevant. Distractions must be eliminated if goals are to be accomplished. Clinebell's comment regarding eliminating distractions is "interrupt panic reactions and regressive snowballing by helping the person face and deal with the issues and explore the alternative approaches to his problem."[12]

In summary, therapeutic flow parallels sales flow: (1) establish rapport, (2) lay out goals and decisions, (3) mobilize the client's resources for coping, and (4) terminate both situational and psychological distractions.

V.
Presentation

The pastor needs a thorough knowledge of the theoretical constructs of the gospel and a familiarity with its practical limits. This is essential if constructive decisions are to be made and commitments joined. Constructive activities do not just happen.

The successful therapist has a firm conceptual map of human personality, derived from immersion in the theories of Sigmund Freud, Carl Rogers, B. F. Skinner, Eric Berne, and many other approaches. A thorough knowledge of the contours and terrains of human personality and emotional expression is necessary for effective psychotherapy.

Likewise, the minister must have a thorough knowledge and understanding of human nature, theology, Scripture, the sacraments, and the tradition of his or her particular ecclesiastical group. Unless the pastor knows the faith he or she is presenting in the context of the local parish, where ministries range from conversion to community service, the pastor has no presentation to make, no services to offer, and no gospel to proclaim.

The salesperson receives extended training to learn all the qualities and facets of a product. Often this includes a verbatim or canned sales presentation. The initial resistance to change encountered by the salesman is overcome only as the prospect is reassured that his real needs are adequately known and fully appreciated.

Inflexibility, rigidity, or defensiveness in a presentation may occur in interpersonal relationships, in the church or as the new dictionary or encyclopedia is being presented. These reactions toward the salesperson are minimized when he or she has thorough knowledge *and* firsthand experience with the product. Knowledge and experience are the handmaidens of good presentation; one learns to listen while speaking. Thorough product knowledge allows one the freedom to be responsive in a relationship.

The goal of a presentation is to evoke change in behavior (verbal and nonverbal) and attitude (conceptual and emotional). In therapy, Clinebell reminds us of the presentation flow. In terms of the client and presentation, Clinebell observes: (1) "Help him to examine the issues and explore the alternative approaches to his problem."[13] What needs require change and how does he change them? (2) "After alternatives have been explored, help him choose the most promising and then to take at least a small step toward implementing the choice." In other words, as the therapist maintains control, the client is moving toward a closing. Taking the small step is the trial close or small commitment necessary to make the "big decision." (3) "Provide guidance in the form of useful ideas, information, and tentative suggestions . . ."[14] The therapist is called to provide guidance by drawing a conceptual map of the choices that are beginning to take shape. This is a highly conceptual activity, but it aids the client in beginning to control the needs and hopes in his or her life. The client is being guided through therapy to face and to own more of the totality of his or her experience. With such intentional guidance, Carl Rogers claims that a new self-structure is organized.[15] This implies that new personality structures are being organized and that changes in behavior and attitude are being evoked. These need to be symbolized in a closure that affirms the person's newly developed capacity to respond with positive, firm, and continuing activity.

VI.
Trial Close

The trial close is the struggle by which the client determines his or her relationship to new feelings, thoughts, and behaviors. The objective is to ask for small decisions and call for a series of small commitments to new feelings, thoughts, and actions. The reordering of life, whether in therapy, church, or home buying, occurs in the process of small decisions. The working through or the trial close help the client to symbolize small portions of interpersonal experience in a context that is perceived as safe. The intentional flow of small decisions or verbal symbolizations allows the client to integrate new aspects of reality so that a new self-structure emerges. If the working through of small decisions is not attempted, calling for a major decision all at once will cause the client to feel such a "big threat" in the present that he will retreat defensively to a prior attitude or mode of behavior that he has experienced as positive and satisfying.

The pastor and therapist need to present options as opportunities for the parishioner or client to interact in positive and manageable ways. Clinebell suggests that the offering of options stimulates the person's self-reliance and functional competence.[16] The trial close is the method which guides the client in choosing the most promising option, in initiating small steps to implement that choice, and in being self-reliant as he integrates new experiences.

To illustrate—the sensitive pastor, in speaking to a family as prospective church members would not ask, "Well, do you want to join Trinity Church?" because that is leading with a big, unmanageable question. The trial close, as it helps to formulate concrete and specific decisions, would offer options that look like this, "Do you think your interest in music would find adequate expression in the church handbell choir?" "Does our family evening (fellowship) supper and worship service meet your family's needs to spend more time together?" or "Would Greg be interested in joining the junior high volleyball team?"

VII.
Closing

Many promising presentations never complete their flow. A presentation has not occurred unless a closing or closure is experienced and celebrated. Many pastors carry a presentation to the point that both parties know what the pastor wants to ask, but these pastors cannot bring themselves to call for a commitment; they collapse emotionally, losing control of themselves and the opportunity for the parishioner to say yes. These pastors have not developed the ability to express pastoral assertiveness in asking for a closing or calling for a decision which would also guide the relationship toward a mutually constructive ending. The reason is simple. They fear rejection. Over the long term they will experience even more rejection, defeat, and self-doubt, but the immediate gain of avoiding rejection and hostility is positive and satisfying.

The therapist is trained to respond to rejection, hostility, and affection that the client uses to avoid closure; that is, to avoid choosing promising alternatives and acting on them. Perhaps more than sales or clergy personnel, the therapist is trained to deal with objections and resistance to closure. Technically these objections are known as transference and resistance. Roughly speaking, transference is an attitude developed toward the therapist that may be affectionate or hostile. Transference is not based upon the actual situation but was originally directed toward another person or situation. The best way to handle transference is to accept and understand and to interpret the reaction or objection in order that a more realistic reaction will take place.[17]

The salesperson is trained to ignore early objections—that is sales language for acceptance and understanding. Neither therapist nor salesman buy into transference. They are not going to be sold or seduced into adopting emotional reactions and patterns of relating that were originally directed toward other persons or situations. On hearing objections of the transference type, one realizes that they are not based upon the present situation. Having accepted transference efforts, the therapist is in a position to press for a meaningful decision based on present relationships.

Resistance and objection must be recognized by the therapist, salesperson, or pastor as the other's efforts to turn down a closure that calls for small, manageable decisions. These ways of avoiding manageable decisions need to be resisted by the pastor. This is accomplished as one moves beyond the client's anxious and distorted efforts to close prematurely by selling the pastor his or her transference. If that occurs the other overthrows the presentation flow and takes control. Then control is based on anxious and distorted objections and not promising choices for growth. This is the net result if one is drawn into and buys the other's defenses. A closing has indeed occurred, but it is not based on the actual situation.

The pastor is often reluctant to resist openly objections that come from the anxiety and transference needs of the parishioner. Such a pastor is not secure enough in himself or in his ability to control the situation to respond initially with acceptance and understanding. A strong pastor, however, will continue to press the parishioner to choose alternatives that are perceived as mutually promising.

The parishioner, in facing his immediate problems, will also have real objections and difficulties. These must be encountered honestly and openly. The pastor endeavors to respond to real objections with his own resources *and* those of the parishioner. One does not focus on the transference *per se* but presses on to the real, here-and-now choices in order that constructive and satisfying decisions will be made. Since transference and the slippery interpersonal dynamics that it generates is the most difficult dimension of the psychotherapist's training and work, it is not surprising that many among the clergy find it difficult to bring a person to choose the most promising alternative. If the pastor has not worked through the theological and psychological dynamics of transference and resistance he or she will be unable to close a deal or effect a decision on the options available to the other party. These ministers will come to fear the no whether the objection is real or distorted. And when they become intimidated the roles reverse themselves. The parishioner or prospective member is in control, leading the fearful pastor into buying any objections that surface as being real and of positive value.

A real objection may be expressed when a prospective church member says to the pastor at St. Paul's, "I do not want to join your church because last Sunday, when I visited, two-thirds of the congregation were over sixty-five, and I want my children to be raised in a church where there are young people.'' If the prospect has correctly perceived the age distribution of the congregation, including a lack of young couples and children, there is a valid objection. This objection has to be faced honestly and openly. This means that the pastor needs to explore with the prospect the real advantages *and* disadvantages of joining St. Paul's. If disadvantages continue to outweigh advantages, the pastor closes the deal and may even suggest other church options for the Joneses. In this instance the pastor has called for a no decision. Both parties have mutually agreed that the relationships and possibilities at St. Paul's are not what the Joneses need or want.

In contrast, had the Joneses inaccurately perceived age distribution, by assuming that the older pastor reflected the congregation's average age, transference or distorted surface objections would be the issue. Perhaps the pastor is already self-conscious and uptight about his advancing years and his effectiveness among couples young enough to be his children. Considerable skill will be required in using trial closes that minimize transference and press for a decision that is based on new self-structures growing out of the encounter.

In ministry, as in therapy and sales work, closings are always being negotiated, alternatives explored, and options offered. Whenever a session ends, a conversation concludes, or a pastoral call terminates, a closing has occurred. Decisions have been made, options selected, and behaviors and attitudes changed. The therapist fully realizes the profound power struggle going on as transference and resistance are transformed into a new self-structure. If the pastor or therapist fails to maintain control at the closing, all is for naught.

The dynamics of good presentation follow the same lines as good therapy and good pastoral care. Pastors need to be assured that the same principles that make for good therapy and presentation will also enable them to close if they deal honestly with real objections and call for decisions that allow positive alternatives to be implemented as they emerge.

The therapist is trained to gain closure on the relationship. So too, the effective minister is intentional about closing when he or she calls for decisions.

Conclusion

We turn now to Part III illustrating three practical areas of parish ministry in which pastoral assertiveness is valuable. In each area presentation flow provides the organizing principle. As demonstrated in this chapter we believe that therapy, like pastoral care, is effective only as the person in ministry can call for a decision that guides the other to choose an option *and* to take the necessary steps to implement that decision.

Raising money for the church, recruiting parishioners for leadership positions, and managing church meetings are three areas of great difficulty because clear and concise decisions are essential. These activities call most decisively for intentional, skillful, and therapeutic use of pastoral assertiveness.

PART III

CHAPTER 8

MEETINGS THAT MATTER

"Committee meetings are a bore. Why do I have to go to that church meeting again? It's a waste of my time."

So the familiar funeral chant about too many church meetings is sounded once again. But meetings are never simply meetings. They can be disasters, or they can achieve goals. Because meetings matter, the pastor or leader must know the dynamics involved and how to handle them in responsible and creative ways.

Effective meetings employ the same intentional dynamics as good counseling. Administrative and personal decisions may seem worlds apart, but they are not. Whereas administrative decisions appear to relate more to external, formal, and housekeeping agenda, and counseling decisions more to internal, informal, and emotional agenda; the truth of the matter is that all decisions proceed from formally stated *and* informally or intuitively perceived interests. These may range from emotion-laden to matter-of-fact proposals and from highly personal to very general programs.

Meetings and personal interests are so closely related that many people act to protect their emotional vulnerability and investment by pretending that meetings don't matter very much—that they are boring and a waste of time. But such persons are already deeply and even defensively related to a meeting. Their negative feelings and fears create an atmosphere in which both emotions and decisions stampede wildly. Thus, we argue that an intentional presentation (flow) is as useful to pastors in church meetings as it is to therapists and salesmen in their contexts. This principle helps the leader or chairperson to guide and direct using a process that openly calls for decisions and affirms both the emotional and intellectual energy involved. Meetings do matter to individuals and congregations.

I.
Have a Purpose

A formal meeting needs a formal agenda. It needs intentional guidance if purposes are to be expressed and goals attained. If the leader cannot or will not set a formal agenda, the event may be regarded as casual conversation; or, there may actually be a captive group manipulated to legitimize someone's private goals.

If there is no openly stated agenda for a meeting, there is no way to measure progress of fulfillment of goals. What does the pastor want to accomplish at a meeting? Frequently, answers to this question are altogether too vague. Typical responses, such as "I'm trying to do my part," "I hope to do the Lord's work," or "I want to see about the building and grounds," are anything but adequate.

Anytime a layperson or pastor goes to a meeting, he or she needs to have a crystal-clear goal in mind, one that can be stated in a brief sentence like, "We're going to decide whether or not to paint the church." The salesman would feel rather silly standing on a front doorstep undecided about why he was there, not knowing his specific goal, and pastors and laypersons *should* also feel embarrassed when they do not know or are not interested in knowing the precise purposes of the meetings they attend.

A. *Leaders Need to Claim Goals.* To be effective, a leader has to acquire the self-discipline to state clearly and concisely the purpose of the meeting and his or her personal agenda as a participant. Some persons argue that the leader, convener, or chairperson should not have or claim a personal agenda or investment. But in reality, human beings cannot disengage themselves from their thoughts and feelings and assume so-called neutral leadership roles.

To believe that the leader can or really wants to attain some ideal of detachment is cruel and inhumane in its excessive demand for neutrality. A leader has a personal agenda, and it must be acknowledged. As church leaders we need to learn to claim our agenda, clarify it, and work with it. The pretense of denying personal agenda will cause that agenda to sabotage both the leader and the meeting.

If a leader cannot reduce his or her goals to a simple sentence, then he is not ready to lead. Perhaps he should not be at the meeting. Or, if the group is unable to state its formal, external agenda, perhaps it too should dismiss, saving everyone time and energy.

In the local church, leaders of various committees, commissions, and boards are selected for terms of one to two years. When these bodies meet once a month or only once every other month, it is important that the function and basic agenda for that committee or board be determined before each session.

If the agenda and function are not stated "up front," much of the year is wasted attempting to discover what that function should be. By the year's end, the committee has formalized a few goals, but with reelection, a new set of people come together to repeat the sorting-out process all over again. Small wonder local congregations and national church bureaucracies are in constant crisis and have low morale about effective ministry and meetings.

Private and hidden interests come to the discussion table hand carried by each member. The committee cannot and should not always deal with private concerns publicly. But, the leader must be prepared to use private interests to help achieve goals claimed by the group or, if necessary, to diffuse them when they interfere.

Once purposes are clearly stated, the leader is in a position to determine what results are realistically attainable. If the insurance salesman knows of an opportunity to sell a ten-thousand-dollar policy, he is in a position to determine whether he can or will accomplish the specific sale. Similarly, the pastor with a stated agenda can calculate the results of the goal to be achieved.

B. *Groups Need to Claim Goals.* Out of the abundance of individual purposes a "corporate" or "group" purpose needs to unfold. This mutual goal can be displayed on newsprint before the group so that each member can consciously own it as a personal objective.

Until the group achieves a common purpose there is no legitimate ground upon which it can proceed. However, if the group proves impotent and ineffectual in its own proceedings, the leader is thereby given a license—or blessed by default—to utilize the group to further his or her private agenda. If the group cannot or will not act to claim and thereby control its goals, its freedom and its power are in danger of slipping away.

This stand-in tactic is clearly a loss for the group because a significant opportunity is missed for leadership and ministry. But decisions have to be made somehow and by someone if goals are to be accomplished.

II.
Homework Needs to Be Done

It pays the pastor or chairperson to have good pre-approach information. Knowledge acquired in advance about the group betters one's chances for accomplishing purposes.

To start with, and this may sound like a simple matter, *know the names of the people in the group.* Name tags, no matter how attractive, only cause people to look down and stare, grasping awkwardly for a name. The effective pastor moves beyond the tag. With fluid confidence he or she mingles throughout the group speaking to and calling each person by name. A name is a trusted possession, and people respond more quickly and more positively to people they like and trust.

Find out about the unique qualities that each member brings to the meeting. Know about the skills, capabilities, weaknesses, dreams, fears, and hopes of each group member. Be sensitive to time and commitment limits. All this information is a resource bank to draw upon when the effort is made to close objectives, to create a meeting that matters.

Does this strategy sound bizarre—not like a church meeting should be? Perhaps to the naive and uninitiated, but we contend that in the name of effective pastoral leadership this type of strategy is valid and germane. This kind of sensitivity and intentionality has been the heart of a vital church community since Jesus called Andrew, Peter, James, and John from their fishing nets. Clergy personnel and laity need to prepare for all meetings, developing their pre-approach in order to process the formal meeting agenda with sensitivity.

III.
Approach

Begin intentional guidance before the meeting. In one-to-one interactions just before the meeting, the leader makes it known that he is present to lead and negotiate with specific expectations of the people and the occasion. *The leader will lay out the agenda immediately and do it with assumptive confidence: be loose and casual; use names; be enthusiastic.*

A formal meeting is not the occasion for generalized goodwill, nurture, and support. If the pastor or leader intends to influence directions, he cannot afford to acquiesce by dissolving specific goals in a general discussion. The pastor needs to claim for himself the benefit the committee or congregation will receive because he leads. This intentional enthusiasm is caring and selling.

"Assumptive confidence" has a quiet side too that encourages people to relax and catch on to new concepts or programs. This quality of confidence does not overwhelm, it allows space for each individual.

IV.
Getting Things Started

A. *Setting-up begins long before the meeting is convened.* Any and every kind of influence the leader can bring to bear on the objectives to be presented should be considered, such as, ordering agenda items, assessing likely vote outcomes, encouraging speeches, and third-party recommendations.

Further, if the leader wants the meeting to be very formal he might wear a three-piece suit and tie or she, an expensive linen ensemble. In contrast, a casual setting may be set-up with informal dress and a cup of coffee in one's hand.

Room arrangement cannot be overlooked for it is vital in the perception of the leader's power and presence. The leader needs a chair that is the "power seat." If no single power location is apparent, the room should be rearranged until one exists so that the leader can occupy that place. In this way, the leader asserts his leadership from the beginning.

In the early stages of the meeting, the pastor or leader makes decisions for the group in small ways. Later when the big decisions come along, the committee is already accustomed to going along with the leader and is comfortable with the quality of the decision he or she inspires.

For example, in greeting people the pastor can assist them to seats of his preference. He observes that it would be helpful if everyone had a pad and pencil. He asks George to locate and distribute these items. He urges Helen to bring her chair closer into the group. Finally, the leader can suggest, if necessary, that it would be better to wait a few minutes until everyone arrives before taking up the matter at hand so that at the right time he can signal for the meeting to begin.

In summary, the members of the group need to be accustomed to the pastor taking the lead in decision-making. It they support an active leadership on seemingly insignificant matters, they will tend to support the leader's sense of direction and purpose when decisions of major consequence are made.

B. *Be certain that the decision-makers are present.* One does not proceed to call for a group decision if the "power brokers" are absent. The rest of the group will not decide without them and once they arrive, discussion will have to begin anew.

In a particular church women's association, the pastor worked energetically to persuade the members to underwrite a summer camp project for retarded children. After a convincing presentation of the pros and cons, there was only one logical choice—members championed no other cause. Funds were in the treasury, and a clear majority favored the project. Despite overwhelming agreement, the pastor could not secure a commitment. Each time a vote was called, someone would insist that they "ought to think it over a little longer," and immediately all the members would agree.

Later, the pastor discovered that a very influential woman made all the big decisions for the association. Because Mrs. Smith was absent that day, the group was totally unable to move ahead. But she was present for the next meeting when, with little discussion, she nodded her approval. The group immediately called for a vote, and the summer camp project passed unanimously.

C. *During the preliminaries it is necessary to eliminate distraction.* The pastor controls the flow by focusing the individual or group on the agenda. Failing to do this, he may find a crop of distractions thwarting thoughtful decision when he calls for the critial response or closure.

Children, for example, can be disruptive influences. One salesman, who worked in a neighborhood with many young children, took his wife with him each day. Her sole assignment was to handle the children. She would literally take control by moving them to another room or outside, so her husband could more easily make his presentation. The lesson is clear: provide for child care during church meetings. The leader should keep distractions from becoming direct influences on final decisions, whether they be children, phones, or janitorial services.

Furthermore, the pastor should eliminate blockages produced by irrelevant materials inserted into the meeting context. (1) Make a printed agenda available from the beginning of the meeting and stick to it. If conversation moves away from the agenda, return the flow to the primary concern. (2) Be ready to call discussions and activities out-of-bounds when they go beyond the purpose of the meeting. Refuse to deal with extraneous areas that cannot be controlled. (3) If a legitimate concern is introduced that lies outside the scope of the meeting, refer or defer the matter. A straightforward response—"No, we are not here to deal with that issue"—will prove helpful.

D. *The preliminaries are an opportunity to establish rapport.* At this point, it is essential for the leader to be attentive and responsive to other people. Listen to others and be open, both receive and give.

There is no need to disclaim one's self-interest in the establishment of rapport or friendship. Claiming pristine and selfless motives smacks of manipulation and yields isolation, not friendship. True integrity is the open acknowledgment of one's self-interest in relations.

An illustration from another area of church life is helpful here. During most sermons the preacher will offer introductory material in the form of anecdotes or other attention-getters. The speaker wants to establish rapport, to secure a common ground before presenting the substance of his concern. Parishioners do not accuse the pastor of dishonesty or manipulation in this case.

Many pastors find value in beginning all their meetings with a warm-up. Some serve coffee and refreshments; others ask members of the group to share something from their day or their feelings about the particular meeting; still others begin with individual or group prayer. Such interactions encourage members to get in touch with other people's lives and the group's life. The goal is to facilitate communication that is intimate, honest, and open. Using ten minutes to begin a meeting with this type of caring will later save hours of struggle, misunderstanding, and conflict. Where rapport rules, people are free to be open in making decisions.

Once rapport is intuitively perceived, the effective pastor will move with it. Disallowing the meeting to become simply an interpersonal pastime, he or she pulls the group together and moves toward the task with strength and efficiency. The task or agenda for the meeting cannot be allowed to slip out of focus. It is important to know one another and one's task, but the group also needs to move toward accomplishing its objectives.

E. *The location of a meeting affects the outcomes of the committee's deliberations.* When the pastor operates in *his* context, the outcome is generally easier to predict. The pastor's study, church rooms, hospital waiting rooms, and other crisis centers tend to give an initial advantage to the pastor. In living-room settings, the situation is more difficult for the pastor. At the home of the church's leading power broker the meeting may well end with tea and cake. This little social gesture allows the parishioner to display his power and his capacity to close on the pastor and the group. A family member may enter the room and announce, "Time to break; refreshments are ready."

The pastor may be at a youth center, at an athletic event, or on a bus trip. The scene is quite different from a setting which provides either pastor or parishioner with control. This netural or circus-tent situation does not lend itself to easy success based on previous experience. Hence, the pastor needs to be assertive if the encounter is to yield positive and encouraging results. The pastor who fails to be intentional can expect an indecisive outcome.

Meetings are called to make decisions and are not training events for personal growth, but pastors are often confused about this. A personal growth event moves from internal, emotional agenda and calls the pastor to be a facilitator or stimulator. But a meeting called to decide whether to renovate the sanctuary or purchase property for a parking lot deals with external agenda and involves specific, objective consequences. The pastor cannot allow an objective meeting to become involved with internal facilitation or psychological ventilation. Personal growth, valuable and vital as it may be, is not the agenda in administrative or decision-producing meetings.

V.
The Agenda Proper

Successful presentations have an unwavering flow whose order and content do not vary. In one sense, then, a presentation is canned because it is prepared ahead. The Scouting America motto, Be Prepared, applies to the pastor who needs to be informed and ready to act when he or she arrives at the meeting. The pastor who is prepared knows that in the typical flow or processing of formal agenda the leader will:

1. State the purpose of the meeting and personal expectations.
2. Share information pertaining to the purpose.

3. Hear objections and allow discussion and debate to occur.
4. Answer the objections.
5. Close on the obtainable goals.

A good presentation will surface most objections. Leading the committee members, the pastor answers their objections clearly and calmly. If this is done during the presentation, objections will not surface again when the final decision is pressed.

Each time a leader chairs a meeting, someone is leading and someone is being led. The leader's position is precarious but simple: will he lead or will he be led; will he be the buyer or the seller? Either leaders in ministry achieve their goals or they are led and controlled by difficulties that could have been overcome. In order to accomplish the mission of the church, it is critical that her representatives maintain their full capacity to lead.

VI.
Starting to End the Meeting

During the course of the meeting and particularly near the end, trial or preliminary closes are used to determine how near the group actually is to a decision.

In showing a home the real estate salesman asks, "Would this room be used as a study, or would you use it as a guest bedroom?" And again, "How would you arrange the living room furniture?" The prospect becomes psychologically involved in furniture placement. By the time the tour is finished, the prospect has come to visualize a family living there; mentally, the prospect has already become the owner of the house. Using a series of trial closes and asking for step-by-step decisions, the salesperson moves toward an unambiguous and final decision.

Similarly, in a church meeting a pastor asks the worship committee if new choir robes are needed. When the committee responds, "Yes, the old ones are in terrible shape," he follows with the question, "Who would look into this problem?" A committee can more easily handle that decision than the big one of purchasing new robes. Consequently, the pastor leads the group step-by-step through the small, easy decisions until the final decision simply falls into place.

Another type of trial close uses "tie downs." While nodding affirmatively, the pastor makes an assertion, adding a phrase that ties down the decision. For example he might say, "Our parish needs a more effective program for our young people, *don't you agree*?" and then follow with, "It would be worth the effort required if just five kids participated, *wouldn't it*?" People will be indicating a yes and actively agreeing as they become increasingly involved with each step.

Finally, when the leader proceeds to the specific agenda or final decision—"Then set up a committee to start the program, OK?"—is easy to complete and acknowledge.

VII.
Gaining the Commitment

A close consists of obtaining a committee's commitment to a specific goal. A close is receiving a simple yes or no. This decision is what the pastor has wanted all along, but a direct appeal usually meets with a host of defenses and objections. Therefore, the close begins with the subtle nuances of the preliminaries and culminates with the final decision. Closing is what a meeting is all about.

A committee generally prefers to put off action and procrastinate because its members do not like to face the responsibilities that accompany decision-making. Thus, the leader's task is to make it easy for people to say yes. This can be done by taking away the sting or bite of a big yes by introducing it in a series of small yes decisions that *assume the big yes*.

Instead of confronting the education committee with the

issue of having a vacation church school, the pastor might ask the group to decide other questions. Would it be wiser to hold the school early in the summer just after public school is recessed or to wait until August? Would it be better to have the school in the mornings or evenings? Should it include the ninth grade, or would it be better to stop at the sixth grade?

In this way the pastor controls the decision by not asking for a yes or no. *He asks only about the kind of yes.* Options are suggested, but only positive options. "Shall we do it now or later?" "Do you want to be on this committee or that committee?" "Do you want to pledge eight hundred dollars or one thousand?" "Shall we meet at the church or in your home?" If a person wants to object, a significant assertion of will is required to override the assumptions made in the pastor's close.

Obtaining the initial decision is only 50 percent of the battle. Thereafter, the decision must be reinforced. A salesperson always wants the decision in writing and signed by the buyer. A signature makes a decision a matter of record.

It would be well if decisions made in the parish were also signed. In a meeting, committee members could read and sign the minutes taken at the time the decisions are made, instead of waiting to look them over at the next meeting. Whenever possible, these notes should be reproduced on the spot so that each person has a record of the individual and the group decisions. This reinforces the decision and the commitment.

Mental decisions and commitments should be accompanied by some concrete expression. The business community asks for deposits in cash. The pastor needs to ask for deposits in terms of some minimal responsibility. If committee members wind up with no real personal investment in a decision, their commitments quickly fade. Each person who helps construct a decision should be called upon for a personal response in support of that decision within twenty-four hours.

Techniques used by revivalists provide excellent illustrations for meetings and the whole life of the church. From the beginning of the revival meeting people know the preacher is present to close on some decisions. The preacher has something to present and expects results. The *pre-approach* begins weeks in advance as he is heralded as the outside expert who comes to proclaim God's Word. The *set-up* involves intensive small group praying before each revival service invoking God's power to convert sinners.

The sermon is the *presentation.* The *closing techniques* encompass invoking the Almighty in prayer *(appeal to authority),* playing soft music *(establish mood),* asking each person to bow the head and close the eyes *(eliminate distractions),* calling for people to raise their hands for special prayer requests *(ask for only the little decisions),* affirming the risk—"Yes, I see that hand. Yes, there are some more. Praise the Lord." *(Everyone is doing it; you are not alone),* and giving the altar invitation *(It's either yes or no, right now!).*

Once the sinner makes his way to the altar, brothers and sisters who have made "the decision" gather to confirm him in his action and ask him to give testimony *(seal the deal)* about the change in his life. He signs a commitment card *(get it in writing),* which can be referred to when he is in doubt about the decision. Finally, he is encouraged to pray that his close friends will also receive this experience *(obtain referrals).*

Some may find this illustration too vivid. Nonetheless, the effectiveness of the closing cannot be questioned. Mainline Protestant denominations generally have struggled to reject this kind of presentation and closure, failing to realize how many principles of human interaction and commitment they have discarded.

Most services in the major Protestant denominations never close because the churches and their pastors have no closing model. Powerful sermons are preached, yet services end passively, "Shall we stand for prayer?" Pastors and churches need an adequate model. Sales personnel who make beautiful presentations but never call for an order starve.

Pastors and churches with no model of closure commit theological suicide.

Conclusion

Continuing problems in church meetings involve confusion of goals, hesitation about who is in charge, the difference between internal (or hidden) and administrative (or external) goals, and dread and reluctance to call for a decision consciously and overtly.

Meetings always make a difference. What kind of difference they make depends in large measure upon the leader's ability to control the group process in order to establish a presentation flow. A presentation flow format honors the integrity of the individual members and fosters beneficial group process so that manageable, long-term commitments can be secured by the group and the congregation in general.

CHAPTER 9

LEADERS
DEVELOP LEADERS

The pastor must continually take charge of developing church leadership. The effective pastor enlists, recruits, and solicits people to make decisions or commitments to the church for the benefit of the congregation and the community in which it ministers. When developing leadership, the minister functions in a managerial position. Whereas the secular manager develops his team from those on the payroll, the pastor must struggle with an organization composed solely of volunteers. Without monetary forms of power, the pastor needs to develop skill in assertiveness and persuasion to forge leadership commitments in keeping with his parishioners' self-interests.

I.
Being Honest About Needs

The pastor must first be honest. When people are approached to provide leadership for particular tasks or positions, the pastor is asking them for an investment of their resources. It is dishonest to hide the personal nature of this request under an amorphous cloak called the Lord's work. In order to motivate his parishioners, the honest pastor does not need to appeal to a sense of guilt or obligation. This type of negative motivation produces poor results in the long run, depletes morale in the life of the church, and betrays the pastor's insecurity.

The pastor must be assertive. If leaders display any universal characteristic, it is that of taking initiative. The leader does not wait for opportunities to arise, but creates them. As a recruiter, the pastor needs to be assertive and move directly toward the desired goal. "I want to talk to you about our family ministry and what it can mean to you," quickly followed by, "When can we get together? This week or next?" Clear, sharp, incisive! The pastor's confident sense of expectation establishes the importance of the cause and frees the parishioner to make an immediate and personal evaluation of interest in family ministry.

II.
Appeal to Self-Interest

The pastoral leader appeals honestly to the self-interest of the parishioner. He acts like the life insurance representative who says, "If something should happen to you, you want your wife to live in the same manner that she is accustomed to, don't you?" or "You want your children's education to be provided for, do you not?" The answers are obvious. The insurance representative moves directly to the basic realities, self-interests, and desires of husband and wife.

Philip Rieff has declared in *The Triumph of the Therapeutic: Uses of Faith After Freud,* that the era of control by guilt and oughtness is gone. The methods of control by which the "religionist" orders experience are being replaced by releasing devices that are potentially more dialectical.[1] Apart from serious questions about the complete absence of communal values, Rieff's research on interactional motives in Western culture suggests that the era is passing when the pastor commands with a coercive jab—"You ought to have your children in Sunday school." The parishioner may ask why or challenge the pastor with "What's in it for me? Convince me." If the pastor is unable to make a case, his or her ministry stops in its tracks.

Pastors need to arouse and excite persons about teaching opportunities, worship leadership, and program development to such an extent that they do not want to say no.

To tap involvement the pastor has to do a thorough job of gathering pre-approach information. She needs to know the pulse of her community and to capture people's values by showing them how a particular program or ministry will enable them to meet their real needs.

For example, in developing a program for the elderly, one prepares members by helping them get in touch with the fact that they are growing old, that they have aging parents, that they have anxieties about being dependent just as they did as children. Once sensitivity is developed, over half the task is completed. An individual's commitment and involvement is rooted in his or her own field of experience and ultimately in self-interest. This approach is in sharp contrast to a pastor who offers, "We have a lot of older people who need our help." Of course, people may feel good about being needed, but such motivation is not as strong and consistent as *self-interest.* When someone's self-interest is touched, he or she is more responsive.

Self-interest benefits both the parishioner and the pastor. The parishioner, who acts in self-interest and finds fulfillment in his commitment, will discover his self-interest turning into agape, that is, a deeper love and relationship to the congregation and to God. Agape, however, is achieved only after an extended period of self-interested involvement during which ego strength matures and mellows. Agape is the end point and not the beginning of ministerial relationships; only as self-interest is acknowledged and fulfilled does agape bloom. The church more often than not has denied or cloaked the appeal of self-interest by claiming to be solely concerned with sacrificial servanthood. Only by encouraging people to claim their self-interests can the church be responsive to human needs.

III.
Specifics Are Manageable

In calling for a decision or asking for commitment, one must be specific and precise about what is wanted. Generalization, in contrast to specification, produces ambiguity and insecurity. A minister's clear and precisely formulated request sets the stage for a distinct yes or no response by the parishioner.

When recruiting people for a task, spell out the exact assignment. The statement, "I want you to drive the church bus"—not "I'd like you to help the church school"—describes the job. Don't talk generally about the church, its faith, and its mission. Spell out specific relationships and leadership functions. Then people can accept or reject a proposal with integrity. In calling for personal investment or commitment, the pastor has a responsibility to state the exact price demanded. If an automobile salesman says that a certain car costs between seven and eleven thousand dollars, a sale is highly unlikely. The prospect who is serious wants to know exactly how much the automobile costs and what the payments will be. The church, too, needs to employ truth in advertising practices. Pastors need to be honest and specific about their expectations.

A pastor—by education, training, and faith commitment—has already invested in the church's mission. Lay people do not share a pastor's total commitment and need to know how to respond in precise and distinct ways with specific limits of time and energy. The pastor needs to tell them in what manner they may become servants of the gospel of Jesus Christ.

IV.
Match Skills and Task

Too often the church operates on the warm-body theory. The pastor working from this theory simply fills vacancies with any warm body that is available and the volunteer's skills and abilities are not considered. The maxim "Better somebody than nobody" rules the day.

We challenge that theory. When there is guarded goodwill or a feeling on the part of the volunteers that they have been coerced into agreement, they have not been placed in ministry. Wrong people in wrong places will quickly ruin any organization, and the situation is no different in the church. This type of mismanagement produces destructive results in well-intended church programs. The congregation eventually loses the volunteer (lacks job satisfaction); the need remains unmet; and the pastor ends up frantically pinch-hitting in all jobs, doing whatever needs to be done to scrape by.

Gazing upon his multiple charts and organizational structures, the better-somebody-than-nobody pastor gloats over having names in each job slot. The denominational executive may be impressed as well. The charts masquerade for reality, they aren't functional, and people are not in loving ministry. This is ministry at its lowest common denominator—sheets of paper and people buried in annual reports.

To maximize rewards, people should be matched with projects for which they have or show both enthusiasm and skill. For example, church hierarchy says that every local church is supposed to have a world-missions committee. If a congregation rejects that concept, the annual report should show this committee scratched as a line item. In an accompanying statement, the negative response should be explained as a lack of interest or as a specific theological position, rather than a lack of funds or members. That is organizational, emotional, and theological integrity.

If a congregation shows interest in the mission committee but has no action to log at annual report time, it could be that the program failed because the pastor was a poor leader. Perhaps he did not have the skill to call for a yes or no decision from the congregation. In that case maybe the pastor could be scratched as a line item. That is integrity too.

V.
Commitments Are in the Present Tense

When a pastor recruits a parishioner or a prospect, he or she needs to ask for commitment to something specific and controllable. A valid commitment is to a present situation because the future is nothing but empty words.

In sales work, this dynamic of deferring into a vague future is called the "be back." A prospect may fall in love with a piece of property, think the price is fine, and have no objections, but still not want to secure the deal with a check. She claims that she will be back later with the deposit. There is nothing wrong with this course of events if the salesman *knows* that he does not have a deal. Psychologically, the salesman may want to believe he has sold the prospect but if he believes this he is only fooling himself. When the prospect returns (statistically speaking she probably won't), the salesman will have to sell her all over again. If she were sold in the present tense, she would buy now. If she doesn't follow through in the present, it is because she has not decided and is not committed materially.

Commitments in the parish need to be in present tense as well. Only the most gullible pastors expect action when the promise is stated in similar terms: "I intend to start coming to church"; "I'll work in the Sunday school soon"; "When the kids get older I will. . . ."

A commitment made in the past does not represent current life either. Commitments need to be constantly renewed or canceled. If a farmer ceases to make mortgage payments on his property, the lender immediately steps into the picture and forecloses on the farm. A foreclosure means that the conditions of the relationship have not been sustained and that the mutual commitment is terminated.

The church could be as straightforward. Peoples' names appear on membership rolls year after year without any review or evaluation confirming that the persons' original commitments are still alive and vital. A church of this nature resembles a community that records no deaths, only births.

One particular church erases its membership rolls each year in January. Members renew their original commitments by rejoining the congregation. This provides the assurance that thirteen-year-olds or anyone with a once vital commitment will periodically reevaluate his membership throughout the whole of his life. A commitment must be alive *now*.

Life changes, people change, and commitments change. Yet church rolls continue to register five to six hundred members when only two hundred persons are active. To rationalize the discrepancy, churches concoct the accommodating category of inactive members. We suspect that commitment or effective ministry and worship do not exist for the inactive member. However, many pastors continue to report higher and higher membership figures that are not based on theological and psychological closure or commitment.

The concept of a renewable church membership offers two significant benefits. First, persons reencounter and reassess their commitments on a periodic basis. And secondly, the church calls for a clear present tense decision on the part of its members, either to maintain the mutual commitment or to terminate the relationship, affirming the integrity of all concerned.

Conclusions

Leaders develop leaders by reaching closure in interpersonal relationships and in opportunities for ministry. Indeed all pastoring is related to interpersonal relations, but leaders are not developed in just any context; *it takes a leader to develop leaders.* Recruiting, enlisting, and enrolling all take place outside the office setting; therefore, the pastor must take personal initiative, and people will respond of their own volition. An activity accomplished in the field, such as developing leaders, is a high risk venture because of the various institutions, organizations, and value systems that compete for each individual's commitment.

The minister ventures forth to the territorial domain of the parishioner or prospect who is not fully persuaded he or she wants to make a leadership commitment to the church. The pastor has to go after that individual to establish a mutuality that serves both the pastor's goals and the interests of the parishioner.

Unfortunately, most training in pastoral care does not help the minister to recruit and develop leaders. Having been abandoned by formal instruction at this juncture, ministers have been forced to develop their skill in pastoral assertiveness and guidance by sheer determination. This chapter offers principles and skills that assist the leader to structure the skills needed for pastors to develop church leaders.

CHAPTER 10

MONEY BELONGS WITH THEOLOGICAL VALUES

Many pastors are openly hesitant and resistant about bringing talk about money into church conversations. When someone raises the issue they feel guilty and embarrassed: "I know I shouldn't be discussing money" or "I know we should be doing the work of the Lord." These pastors rationalize their lack of assertiveness by claiming that financial matters belong to the domain of the money experts or the business community because the work of the church is not based on an ideology that gives money power. These ministers avoid the entire range of opportunities available to the church and to the congregation when money commitments are given to the church and put to work by the pastor.

This attitude is equally entrenched in the mind of the laity. They become as apprehensive as the pastor when the topic of money arises. Thus, on the infrequent occasions when the pastor advances money matters, parishioner anxiety often escalates into hostility: "How come every time I go to church they are asking for more money?" The pastor and congregation who harbor such defensive attitudes fail to exercise pastoral care in the area of financial commitment to the claims of Jesus Christ in the local congregation and in the witness of the denominational boards and agencies.

Because of this defensiveness about financial stewardship, denominational representatives are frequently resented for what appear to be designs on local church funds. But the need for a wider ministry is legitimate. Local pastors too often become trapped in developing new programs and in promoting special worship and service opportunities, but neglect to place these programs in a financial perspective. The end result is that the significance of money in a person's commitments is overlooked. We argue that financial expenditures are evidence of internal belief.

Consider an illustration of this principle. Accounting regulations in the real estate industry do not permit a company to book a sale unless 10 percent of the sale price is on deposit. There may be a signed contract, an oral understanding, a meeting of the minds, or some other form of acceptable agreement, but *cash* must change hands. For a sale to be recognized, accounting rules require the purchaser to lay out his money.

Before an automobile dealer will hold a car, he asks for money down. He knows he is not secure until words are verified by material commitment.

"Earnest money" is a sensitive subject for pastor and parishioner and it embarrasses and discomfits many in the church. When members join they receive a church packet with articles on the history of the denomination and the local congregation. Usually a membership directory, a theological statement about the beliefs of the church, and sometimes a pledge card will be enclosed.

Some pastors end their presentation here, thus relinquishing the opportunity for pastoral care in this area of life. The effective pastor expects fiscal accountability on an annual basis—"I haven't received your pledge card yet." Unfortunately, this call for accountability is the exception rather than the rule. Financial accountability needs to be recognized as a standard opportunity for pastoral care in the local church.

I.
Dollars Are Values

Dollars reflect one's values; they demonstrate the location and extent of commitment. There is nothing unchristian about this; in fact, money and commitment are inseparably connected. As one perceptive pastor notes, "Show me where a man spends his dollars, and I'll show you where his commitments are."

If ambiguity and guilt are taken out of the money issue in the church, everyone benefits. First, a sound and healthy budgeting structure can be established. Second, the pastor will have a clearer picture of the components of ministry and their costs, and he will be able to talk about money without embarrassment. Finally, parishioners will understand that they can utilize money as a mechanism to clarify and express their values and commitments.

Dollars indicate a parishioner's theological and emotional values. Referring to laypersons as $100 Christians, $1,000 Christians, or $5,000 Christians, would be strange and undesirable, and this kind of labeling need not happen, but parishioners do need to claim the result of their values. They need to be able to make a positive value statement, "My tithe supports inner city work" or "My contribution enables the new building program." Church members need to understand that their giving reveals and creates inner conviction and pastors need to appreciate this, too.

When the parishioner presents his money in terms that are personally significant, he is in a psychological position to experience his faith coming alive. Positive expectations deepen and enrich the meaning of one's faith.

Giving money to the home church is an expression of service and trust in local, national, and international ministries that truly enlivens the donor. The church member, who fails to give or who gives without claiming the issue of money, misses specific and concrete reminders of how religious values are offered and received through the church.

Pastors need to close for cash. People do not give to support an abstraction or to some ecclesiastical void where their money and lives disappear. People will not pay to support abstract benefits. People pay because they know they are supporting specific and actual activities across a whole range of local congregational and denominational ministries. They pay because there is a heightened sense of mutuality—of strengthening and being strengthened, of leading and being led. They pay because a pastor or a layperson talked money. They pay because giving money allows theological values and faith to be created corporeally in the church.

II.
Money and Internal Satisfaction

A pastor once set up a "care-team" ministry. Each volunteer was asked for a commitment of four hours every Wednesday evening and twelve additional hours each week. The pastor extolled the benefits of this experience to his parishioners, but there was a unique twist to his promotion. Each participant would pay one hundred dollars tuition for the program even though no direct costs were involved for the church.

Enrollment was immediate, and volunteers came with checkbook in hand. Expectation and commitment were high as shown by the presentation of money. People arrived early for every session and lingered afterwards.

All of this did not come about because people paid for the program. The care-team ministry had other benefits, but the participants concluded that paying enhanced the experience. This paying motif became a model for many other programs in the same parish. It was accepted and became a satisfying norm in the life of that church.

The Rolls Royce owner will usually admit that a five thousand dollar Ford could fulfill his transportation needs as adequately as the hundred thousand dollar Rolls. Value is not measured solely in terms of external utility because internal rewards and satisfactions are more important than functionality. Incorporation of this dynamic exists at the heart of the church situation described above.

When a pastor operates away from the office, he has to proclaim the gospel (the meanings and values of the faith) through symbols that people in the field understand. Money is one of those symbols. The man in the street knows the import of "You get what you pay for." Today's pastor needs to employ this symbol to create theological and service values for parishioners.

For years pastors and churches carry people on their rolls who do not value that relationship. People must be challenged to clarify their relationships and commitments to the church. There is no middle ground whereby they can feel good without some form of investment or value. It's either yes or no with themselves and/or their pocketbooks.

One may consider the "paid membership" plan as one component of church funding. In this plan, the ego is challenged to develop values for itself and the church by giving money. If the church fails to engage and create one's values at this level, another level for engagement remains open—the tax shelter. Giving, organized around the tax shelter plan, admits to mutual self-interest, recognizing that benefits are being mutually encountered. Such honesty helps to reinstill integrity in church finances and frees the church to move away from guilt as a motive for giving.

III.
A Diversified Ministry

The sensitive pastor recognizes that people's needs differ. Because of this variation people are interested in different forms and expressions of the gospel. The pastor's goal remains the same: gain a commitment that will meet the need of the parishioner and serve the church.

Sensitivity to needs is illustrated by a national publishing firm that sends out thousands of college students each year to sell books door-to-door. Each student carries samples that include several different types of books: dictionaries, Bibles, medical texts, educational works, and children's readers. These volumes vary in price range as well. The students are trained to listen to the need of the prospect and to sell to that need. If a mother wants a storybook for her child, the student is trained not to insist upon selling her a medical text!

A church budget does not often have this flexibility. Generally parishioners must buy the whole thing (make a blanket pledge) or not at all. But if options are made available, the pastor can ask, "Where do you *want* to put your money?" The answers obtained would identify the congregation's real concerns.

There is the risk that some projects would receive funds while others would not. An initial failure to raise money for a specific project would be an instructive and manageable test. The church financial leaders who are responsible, could employ the trial close procedure to determine whether the congregation-at-large is confused or misinformed about the project; or, whether the objections (failure to fund the budget) are surface reactions *or* real objections. The trial close may call for going back to the drawing board. Instead of giving up, this procedure allows pastors and lay leaders to learn to be more specific and informed in their presentation and to call for small decisions as ways of establishing the financial commitment of specific concerns that the congregation has identified.

With confident use of trial closes, the congregation and the individual parishioners come to own the programs and ministries they are willing to fund with the monetary yes *and* to arrive at a reasonable understanding of why they say no to other theologically relevant projects in a given budget year.

It is essential to maximize specific program funding over against undesignated giving. A certain percentage should be set aside for basic expenses. From there the people's priorities should determine the budget. People rebel, either emotionally or by withholding positive interest and funds, when they are forced to give to projects of which they disapprove. They contribute more than dollars when they select their programs; they contribute their lives and long-term commitment. Budgeting for a diversified ministry allows for individual discretion and increases a parishioner's giving and commitment.

With a diversified program, the pastor can seek support from nonmembers for community-oriented programs that are of mutual benefit. Furthermore, one never has the problem of stale and outmoded ministries because when support dries up for an individual program that program is killed.

Much of the church's potential for mutually satisfying ministries is lost because pastors and governing boards insist that each member give equal support to each and every church program.

IV.
Illegitimate Funding

The person with the most dollars is not necessarily more knowledgeable about the life of the local church, and therefore, the moneyman should not control how dollars are spent, although he certainly has a voice.

At this juncture the legitimate guiding function of the pastor is called into action. The financially powerful parishioner does not necessarily have a keener sense of the "mind of the Lord" than the poor widow. Thus, his influence on priorities should not dominate all funding and program decisions. This means that the wealthiest layperson does not always know what is best in terms of the ministry of that congregation.

Control of the budget belongs to the congregation in general. The pastor—along with the governing board of the congregation—needs to retain a measure of control in order to insure a successful presentation of corporate values.

If a wealthy widow wants to own and dictate the church's ministry, the pastor and congregation need to tell her no deal. For instance, the wealthy widow may support 50 percent of a twenty thousand dollar budget, and she may want to have her ten thousand spent entirely for landscaping. The pastor needs to reply, "We aren't selling just that here. Maybe some other church down the road would be glad to oblige you."

The effective pastor promotes designated giving but controls the boundaries of that giving. If he does not maintain some measure of influence, the wealthy or loud parishioner may quickly gain undeserved and inappropriate control while the pastor and congregation simply tag along. While the big giver may intimidate most pastors, he or she must be challenged nevertheless, or the church runs a risk of complete monetary seduction.

Funding of illegitimate projects needs to be called out of bounds or labelled not sold here. *The test of a pastor's strength is whether or not he can turn money down at the crucial point in the power struggle!* If he can and does, he keeps his power and maintains the integrity of the church and her mission to witness to the revelation of Jesus Christ its Lord.

V.
Matching Ministry and Parishioner

It is important for the pastor to realize that the dynamics are the same both for ministries requiring large sums and for those requiring small ones. The same amount of knowledge about opportunities for ministry and about parishioner needs is required in closing on a small commitment as on a large one. When the parishioner is capable of supporting a substantial ministry, why settle for a small one?

Most commitments are small because pastors are afraid to ask for large ones. Once a pastor had the occasion to ask for a ten thousand dollar donation, and his seeming audacity, because the individual made the commitment, paid off.

When the program is important, it is poor leadership and stewardship to accept a small commitment if the parishioner is capable of a substantial one. It behooves the pastor to have good background information on the financial capabilities of the parish.

VI.
Non-Dollar Value Symbols

Dollars are not an exclusive symbol of one's faith commitment. Christian ministry and service are also ego-expressive activities. Expression may be in time, energy, work, or any number of other "contribution units." These activities are also properly classified under the category of funding the church. The church could not operate if donations of this type were not made. A widow's mite should have a big voice in the programming of the church, lest big givers try to play games with the church's ministry as some do with their junior executives' futures.

The widow's mite deserves recognition and response for it is offered to the church in loving concern. It may be expressed in many forms: the teen-ager who oversees child care services in the nursery; the mechanic who maintains the church bus; or, the blind woman who plays the organ for regular and special events. However, pastoral confrontation is called for when a parishioner plays the destitute widower character at church while being "Mr. Affluent" at the country club.

VII.
Contexts for Fund-Raising

Earlier we outlined three settings of pastoral care: the office-medical context, the living room or different culture context, and the circus tent context. Fund-raising is a legitimate part of pastoral care, and it takes place in each of these settings. It follows the classic format of the psychotherapeutic relationship and of the sales presentation.

A. *The office-medical context.* A banquet is a typical arena for fund-raising in the church. Because the context assists and provides control, we understand it to reflect the office-health model. One church that employs this technique invites its key members to a fund-raising dinner where the solicitation team has control of the context in both its entertainment and presentation.

Use of the fund-raising meal requires a good presentation flow. Pre-approach, approach, and set-up are the positive givens for the committee. Concentration is on the *content* of the presentation—the soft sell approach—and great care is exercised in detailing trial closes so that the specific options of the church's potential ministry for the upcoming budget year will play across the theological imaginations of the dinner guests. During the closing, the call for a financial commitment is low key as a consequence of the interest issuing from the congregation's life in specific programs.

A fund-raising committee must not manipulate or control with a heavy hand. A canned presentation, a stacked setting, and unrelenting pressure may contrive a situation that produces money but fails to encounter persons or their real theological and emotional commitments. The current year's pledge may be captured, but the resentment and resistance such maneuvering arouses is not likely to pass before the next banquet. Because whole persons were not encountered while the dollar was being nailed down, many parishioners will refuse to come near the banquet hall in the years that follow. Persons need genuine encounters if long-term commitments are expected.

B. *The living-room context.* This is the classic and most effective setting for church fund-raising. It is also the arena most threatening and frightening to the majority of church members. Because of this, many parishioners prefer to pledge through the mail or by the less personal banquet.

In this context a good pre-approach is relatively easy, but

one needs to proceed slowly in establishing the approach and set-up. The pastor or visitor does not rush to call for a decision. Rapport and a warm relationship are necessary in bringing budget needs to life in the intimacy of the living room context. The presentation flow will then occur among friends who are comfortable in talking about money. The yes or no response has to be elicited from the parishioner. If the reply is positive, the canvasser immediately closes with the question, "How much?" Calling for the dollar commitment yields measurable results in terms of a clear decision and a specific dollar amount if the decision is positive.

C. *The circus-tent context.* This neutral context calls for a sensitive and perceptive presentation. Here the pastor has to be able to think on his feet and offer alternative options because, while the context is neutral, the setting and rules of procedure belong to the secular world.

Unlike the banquet meal or the house-to-house visitation, this context reaches the critical stage of interaction at the point of asking for money. Pre-approach and approach efforts may be quite minimal, but set-up and presentation will need to be highly adaptable and subject to sudden and radical shifts due to the volatility of circus-tent gamesmanship. Here, conversation flows into the closing but is secondary to the closing itself. The church representative may be bluffed on through the formal presentation and the trial closes with positive gestures. Bluff and playing around with positive responses will only cease as the pastor is prepared to ask for a serious and specific commitment. In effect, the church visitor is calling the bluff of the noncommitted but playfully interested other.

The crafty parishioner and the wily community leader can deflect ministerial ambivalence and imprecision with guiltless and playful joy. Hence, the pastor needs to be explicit about the purpose and goal of the encounter. The presentation should name a specific need (not the whole church program). From the first, the pastor tries to close for a decision and departs as soon as one is reached.

There is no need to beat around the bush or waste valuable time. After a brief greeting, the minister should announce the purpose for the encounter. She could just come out and say, "Ann, we need a hundred dollars per family to kick off our youth retreat fund. It means a lot to the kids. Can I count on you for that hundred?" Or he might suggest without apology, "Joe, we need to buy some new furniture for the nursery, and we don't have funds in the treasury. I know your family appreciates the services, so how about fifty or a hundred dollars to start us off?"

The circus-tent is also the best context in which to obtain referrals. Reaching out to shake hands, in preparation for departure, the alert pastor comments, "Thank you for the donation, Mr. Swanson. Do you have any friends who might feel as strongly as you do about the migrant ministry? They don't need to be members of the church." Another simple request for references could be formulated like this, "Could you help me find some other people who are as committed to this issue as you are?"

Conclusion

Money is a part of church life and pastoral care that is here to stay. We need to recognize, affirm, and control its use.

The investment of money (or time and energy) signifies one's values and commitments. Far from being embarrassing, this concept, when recognized, liberates the lives of pastors and parishioners.

Lay people need to be directed to legitimate values and programs where they can invest their money, themselves, and their theology with integrity and consequence. The pastor, in a very real sense, is a theological investment counselor for the local congregation in its ministry.

PART IV

CHAPTER 11

DYNAMICS OF PASTORAL CARE: LISTENING AND GUIDING

In the previous three chapters we considered three of the basic ministerial functions in the local church that require pastoral assertiveness. Fund-raising, leadership development, and productive meetings depend upon pastoral ministry that is caring *and* selling. These parish activities and dynamics of leadership are typically the most troublesome for the average congregation. Why? Because generally the pastor is trained in and instills among the laity a pastoral care model that either omits or is blatantly ambivalent about assertiveness as an appropriate mode of relatedness among God's people.

Under influence of a "responsiveness" perspective, guidance and control are perceived solely in terms of psychological defensiveness, coercion, and manipulation. However, we argue that guidance and control are always at work in significant interpersonal relationships as exemplified in psychotherapy and parish ministry in general. Further, we maintain that church functions that are intensely interpersonal, such as fund-raising, leadership development, and meetings, call for disciplined control and guidance if ministry is to occur.

The ministry of guidance remains for many pastors and congregations the most perplexing opportunity for faithful witness to the ongoing life of the church and of her Lord, Jesus Christ.

I.
A Perspective on Listening and Guiding

Pastoral assertiveness and pastoral responsiveness are complementary, dialectical dimensions of pastoral care. We illustrate the need and constructive examples for developing pastoral assertiveness as a model for ministry. This model of ministry needs to be located in the overall context of pastoral care and counseling.

Listening and guiding are companion activities in pastoral care and parish nurture.

A. *Listening.* Being able to listen carefully and attentively and then eventually to offer perceptive and meaningful comment is not an innate talent, it is a developed skill and for many one that is not easily acquired. Sensitive listening requires training, practice, and evaluation. Acquiring these skills for ministry involves an arduous apprenticeship.

Many who speak for the church confuse volume, intensity, and quantity of verbal production with genuine communication. Only when the message is given and received, the control mutually understood, and the intended response of command heard clearly, has effective communication taken place. Sensitive listening is a treasure of great worth and is needed in all phases and expressions of the church's ministry.

The maxim—When in doubt, listen—is receiving wide acclaim these days. Listening is a procedure that is only partially understood. But sensitive listening does not mean emotional or interpersonal passivity!

Listening may at first appear to be a passive behavior, but as a skill in ministry and counseling listening becomes very active. Good listening utilizes the basic elements of presentation flow: *control the goal*—decide that listening is the most helpful assistance and plan to listen; *pre-approach* —know the circumstances of the person(s) talking as thoroughly as possible; *approach*—enter the relationship actively in order to listen; *set-up*—establish rapport by being open about wanting to listen and about avoiding distractions that stem from internal impulses or external wisps of activity; *presentation*—show how listening is a value that can meet the parishioner's real needs.

Effective listening may appear passive, but it is also a very intense, alert, engaging, demanding, and controlled activity if done well. Listening is essential to ministry and cannot accurately be understood or perceived as inactivity or inattentiveness.

B. *Guiding.* Unlike listening that seems passive in the immediate context, guiding is associated with notions of active word and deed in the present. At the same time guiding has its passive, receptive, and quiet dimension as well. This passivity occurs in the memorization of Bible stories or verses of Scripture, the computations of budget-planning, and in the countless hours of supervisory conferences. Guiding, if it is to be effective, moves from a strong and secure base of *knowledge, practice, critique, memorization, and comprehension of the minutiae* of budgets, lesson plans, sociological findings, doctrine, and Scripture. Obtaining the ingredients that focus the guiding activity is very much a listening or responsive relationship.

An overall perspective of pastoral care and counseling includes listening and guiding, activity and passivity, immediate and long-range activities and values, internal and external restraints. Guiding and listening are complementary; and each runs the full spectrum of emotional, theological, and behavioral activities. Ultimately, one is not valued above the other; both are essential for ministry through pastoral care.

II.
Transition in Receiving and Asserting

The complementary nature of listening and guiding has been demonstrated and established. These two activities operate in some kind of dialectical balance, and one can claim that these polarities ultimately are related. Our concern ranges beyond arguments about the possible relationship of theoretical entities, typologies, and abstractions. For the person in ministry—lay and ordained—the practical issue is always the day-by-day challenge: "How does it work?" or, "What are the dynamics in the transition from receiving to asserting, from asserting to receiving?"

In the selling model we have a clue: *one invites the other to sell back.* The pivotal point in the transition is the capacity of the pastor to invite, offer, give, and suggest to the other that a relationship is never completed, fulfilled and/or finally affirmed as authentic unless and until the opposite reality (either receiving or asserting) is meaningfully experienced by both parties as they participate in the event.

The transcendent value from which the pastor operates and to which he or she points the various expressions of ministry is a theological truth. God is the extreme instance of both receiving and asserting. God's asserting activity in creation is a reality that most people in the Judaeo-Christian tradition will readily affirm; God's receiving activity in the believer's worship and praise of God is a reality fully as majestic as creation. But, for many, the latter is far more difficult to affirm.[1]

God contains extremes in contrast, embracing the farthest boundaries of asserting power *and* receiving praise and adoration. No one is more capable nor can surpass God's capacity to create *and* to receive praise. This is a given, a constant, an *a priori* in the Judaeo-Christian tradition and its theology. God encompasses the extreme instance of receiving and asserting. Therefore, those seeking to minister in God's name, as children of God, are obliged by their transcendent theological values to participate in the full range of receiving and asserting. Furthermore, *the minister, as a representative of God and God's indwelling presence in the church, has received the authority, power, responsibility, and freedom to invite the other to control back.* In short, we are invited into a covenant relationship and to make a covenant—God and the people covenant together.

If the pastor's dominant mode in a relationship is listening, he or she has the responsibility to invite the other person to listen; when the dominant mode for the pastor is guidance, the individual or group being ministered to is invited to provide guidance that is binding on the relationship. No relationship is fulfilled, nor goals and commitments secured, nor mutuality achieved, until the invitation to exercise control is given and acted upon. The pastor must be able to distinguish between receiving and guiding so that he or she can call for a transition in how the relationship is being experienced. The transition demands great sensitivity and maturity by the pastor. The pastor or priest, called by the living God, is summoned to participate in the lives of others by receiving and asserting.

Further, it is the minister's vocation to complete the initial phase of ministry by calling forth out of the relationship a dynamic shift that will cause that ministry to flow in the reverse direction. The party that initially receives is called to assert, and vice versa. Ministry in the name of the living God is incomplete and fragmented unless the reverse flow in the dynamics of asserting and receiving can be experienced and claimed.

III.
Theological Use of Listening and Asserting

A brief excerpt and commentary on an effort to minister in a hospital setting will illustrate the point above; namely, effective ministry occurs when the invitation to control or sell back is greeted with a demonstrated response. This incident was described by a seminary student in a written contact report. The student preparing the verbatim case study was an ordained clergy of several years, having specialized training and significant experience in crisis ministry in the general hospital setting.

The incident involves a visit to a patient (Henry) whom the minister had come to know over a six-month period. Recently, Henry had been readmitted to a hospital for removal of a tumor on the spine. Successful removal of the tumor had introduced several debilitating consequences, including partial paralysis. In the beginning stages of the relationship, Henry had evidenced a generally depressed and despondent attitude to his retirement. That general despondency, now coupled with paralysis and other painful side effects from the operation, is the background to Henry's very recent but openly expressed desire to die. The minister wrote that his intention was to explore with the patient that desire "and to try to evoke whatever hope there might be."

Throughout the reported conversation the patient expresses ambivalence about wanting to die *and* wanting to live. At one point, Henry shares an idea that perhaps God will bring relief by causing death, but then he says, "I don't think I can ask God to help me die." Henry's ambivalence about life and death also finds expression in his ambivalence about the power of prayer and God. *(What if God were to answer his prayer to die?)* The conversation, however, drifts away from God and prayer as resources for hope. The talk shifts to a concluding exchange about the patient's capacity to achieve some comfort—hope—in his condition. The pastor reports, "I intended to help him work on hope, but he was doing that, in his own way, before I said a word. For example, he had to call my attention twice to the fact that he was sitting up again."

Did the pastor make theological use of listening and asserting? We think not, especially when we read the minister's own words: "Once again, I am learning that the patient always knows best *what* he needs to struggle with and *how* he should go about it."

Two principles from the pastoral assertiveness model suggest that the pastor made little theological use of listening and asserting. He failed to effect the dynamic transition of listening *and* asserting in the relationship. These principles observe that: (1) "The parishioner (or the other) is not *always* right." This dynamic truth is in contrast to the implied, but patronizing, moralism that the customer always knows best; (2) "One invites the other to assert." Neither of these principles of pastoral care were employed.

Positive use of the two principles would have freed the minister from excessive listening and his emotional dependency on receiving and would have allowed him to be a faithful witness to the living Lord who participates fully in listening and guiding, receiving and asserting. With this freedom, one hopes the pastor could have effected a change in the relationship so that a dynamic transition could have occurred in the character of the entire conversation in which the pastor was receiving and listening, and the patient asserting and guiding. If the minister cared enough, he could have employed guidance to pursue Henry's ambivalence about the power of God and prayer to create and end life.

Had he attempted the transition and been even somewhat successful, the pastor could have continued in ministry by allowing the patient to receive and listen and, thereby, experience the fuller power of the reality of the living God to listen *and* guide, to receive *and* assert. In failing to operate from the two principles stated above, the minister lost the opportunity to make dynamic use of the patient's ambivalence about hope and prayer in a theological framework.

And finally, there is an obvious conclusion about the pastor who is supremely committed to the philosophy that the other—patient, parishioner, prospect—always knows best. That pastor is dominated by the responsiveness model of pastoral care and has not begun to understand the theological and psychological dynamics of pastoral assertiveness. Using that model, the pastor is not expressing effective personal or theological care.

IV.
Guiding: The Tender Touch

Listening and guiding are pastoral care correlates; they are dialectical (or dipolar) theological and psychological constructs. Henri Nouwen in *The Living Reminder* endeavors to speak to the three ministries suggested by Seward Hiltner long ago (healing, sustaining, guiding).[2]

To suggest the presence of tenderness in guiding, Nouwen considers the *confronting* and *inspiring* dimensions.[3] These images suggest the tone of our concern throughout this book. Pastoral theology needs to develop a positive view of guiding as a central function of pastoral care and counseling. Three of the components needed for such a recovery shall be briefly considered: rationality as guiding, prayer and sacraments as guiding, and guiding in transference.

A. *Rationality as Guiding.* Emotionalism as a substitute for genuine piety has a long history in American churches. It is evident that the revivalistic and the T-group movements continue to exert considerable influence on the church's ministry. "Trust your feelings" has become a slogan for many. Such appeals have a useful purpose. But careful, reflective study of Scripture, church polity, the church fathers, and current events is equally important. Thorough knowledge, disciplined study, and a thoughtful morality are highly rational aspects of Christian faith and ministry. Their contribution to parish ministry is sorely needed.[4]

The cultivation of rationality is one of the needed functions of the gathered community. Learning may not be a spectacularly evident or flamboyant expression in guidance. But, as in the dynamics of pre-approach, one needs to know the church and theology in order to provide pastoral care. Knowledge allows one to challenge, to be guided into truth, and to be affirmed in the truth.

B. *Prayer and Sacraments as Guiding.* A disciplined life of prayer and meditation, and of being drawn into Scripture, from which the language of prayers and hymns flow, guides one toward truth. By participating in the formal sacramental and liturgical life of the communities of gathered believers, one is guided in a fuller life with and in the Body of Christ. Sacraments are a source of inspiration and confrontation. They are guides through which God invites believers to come back, to make a claim on the Body of Christ. Sacraments guide and assert.

C. *Guiding in Transference.* Transference is the psychological transfer of affection and animosity onto a contemporary person or situation from a previous encounter. Guiding can help to recapture and relive that experience—the original vision and its memories.[5] When *past* memories or emotions are freed, they no longer control *present* debilitating encounters, but instead become guides for new awarenesses that are firmly based on present realities. Guiding invites one to control in return because one has released internal and transcendent resources to exercise guidance. Released memories, in their capacity to guide one through the dynamic exchange of receiving and asserting, provide guidance for the pastor so that he can move beyond the temptation to punish himself and others when they direct emotions and attitudes toward him that only belong to past encounters. The minister can lead the building of a new vision and does not *have to have* submissive (or one-dimensional) parishioners to find satisfaction.

Conclusion

Guiding is a source of inspiration and confrontation for the church. In ministry, the need to recover the lost vision of the positive, inspiring function of guiding is stark. We hope to point toward a rediscovery of the proper theological and psychological dynamics of listening and guiding. The church needs the ministry of pastoral assertiveness that is fully caring, receptive, and receiving.

CHAPTER 12

PERSONAL AND THEOLOGICAL INTEGRITY: LEADING AND BEING LED

We come now to explore the theological dynamics of pastoral assertiveness. We did not omit theological considerations earlier, but the principal focus has been the general categories of experience that relate to guiding. In the final chapter we broaden and focus our analysis on theological dynamics.

First, we will consider the subtle, personal experience of leading and being led. Second, the central theological dynamic of the Judaeo-Christian tradition, that of risking a heightened mutuality, is explored. And finally, we will illustrate the expansive theological dynamic of leading and being led in all experience. Thereby we hope to conclude this study by illustrating guiding as a particular and specialized theological and psychological expression of leading and being led. As a theological principle, guiding is the basis for pastoral assertiveness. In the broadest sense assertiveness, understood and developed as a theological activity, can be claimed as an ontological category. The phenomenon of leading and being led is not a limited category or experience; it is experienced by all of reality.

That claims a great deal, so let us proceed.

I.

The Personal Invitation

We turn again to the selling model for illustration and insight. For the accomplished door-to-door salesperson, the relationship that makes a closing possible is said to occur in a brief fifteen to twenty second interlude at the early stage of the encounter.

Consider for a moment that George, our salesman friend with sample case in hand, is approaching the front door of Mrs. Smith's home. One may assume that she already knows he is in the neighborhood and is on his way to her home; or, when he arrives that she will piece together almost instantly that he is a salesman. George does not have to pretend about who he is or what he does. He approaches, sets the sample case on the door step in full view, and knocks on the doorpost. Instead of waiting hopefully or anxiously for Mrs. Smith to appear, he may turn from the door, perhaps to talk with children, to stroke a pet kitty or dog; or he may walk several steps away from the front door, and with his back to Mrs. Smith's porch, pause to admire the lawn, some flowers, or children playing. Soon a slight sound betrays Mrs. Smith's presence at the door. As yet there is no eye-to-eye direct, personal contact. Mrs. Smith may even need to take initiative to claim curious George's attention.

During the following fifteen second interval an interesting drama unfolds. She calls out to George, "May I help you?" George turns fully toward her—still safely several feet away—and casually, almost with an air of being disturbed from a nap, and confidently replies, "Hello, Mrs. Smith. I am George Jones."

At the end of that brief transaction George may have shifted positions only slightly toward the prospect. Her uncertainty, her suspicion of being ripped off, and her concern for her own safety are being openly challenged by George's warm and friendly presence. George has already led Mrs. Smith but initially, very briefly and very gently. There is a psychological invitation in his positive and reassuring lead because he is intentionally brief. By offering the lead to Mrs. Smith, George is risking all. She is entirely free and has the power to reject him or accept him. And George has invited her to claim that power.

The dynamics of this brief encounter can be summarized as two steps forward and one step back, as leading and being led. Confidence is displayed, not by a boisterous introduction, but by a confidence that is subtle and profound, allowing the other to experience the capacity for leading of the salesperson, the pastor, the therapist, or the parent.

The risk is in inviting the other to experience his or her own strength by taking the initiative in return; now, the other is providing the lead—the other has a degree of strength and control. George is secure enough not to grab for psychological control. He takes a step back sensing that Mrs. Smith will take a psychological step forward to close the relationship instead of moving away. The effort to establish the possibility of mutuality, of leading and being led, either succeeds or fails in less than twenty seconds!

Dramatic perhaps; an everyday occurrence?! Yes indeed! The phenomenon of leading and being led that receives keen attention in the selling model is common to all human interaction, all introductions, all efforts to establish a basis for mature mutuality.

II.
Risking Heightened Mutuality

Mutuality is the more general category of leading and being led. Mutuality does not occur if the dynamics of leading and inviting the other to take initiative are not present. Allowing another to experience the capacity of leading and the invitation for the other person to take two steps forward does not proceed from agreement. Although important activities may be accomplished, agreement is a stalemate in which only low-grade mutuality is present. True or authentic mutuality occurs when the other, Mrs. Smith in the illustration, has the capacity to reject, to grab control, and to dominate.

Risking a significant rejection or rebuff is the beginning of mutuality. The minister has to put psychological and theological content on the line with an invitation. In experiencing vulnerability, George initiated a lead—or the two steps forward. In the pause that followed, an invitation was issued—the lead was handed over as George stepped back. Mutuality may occur as the other experiences the full opportunity of leading in place of being led. The integrity of the minister's risk in offering true psychological and theological power can be reciprocated by the parishioner's risk in taking similar theological and psychological steps forward.

The pastor need not be insecure about who is "supposed" to take the initiative first. We demonstrated this in the discussion of listening and guiding. What matters is that the pastor is secure enough to allow the leading-and-being-led process to unfold, rather than grab for the lead. If the pastor seizes the lead and is unwilling to relinquish it to facilitate mutuality, the struggle to establish closure (or mutuality) will be fought later, and often with greater intensity and crudeness.

Risking heightened mutuality in all of life is a firm indication that personal integrity is being experienced and that the capacity to engage in leading and being led is present in its psychological and theological depths.

III.
The Theological Dynamics
of Leading and Being Led

Guidance, or assertiveness, is both responsive and responsible. It proceeds from a religion-influenced expression of freedom or self-determination. By definition, freedom can mean at least two things. First of all, it is a mode of exerting one's will to the satisfaction of that will. But second, and in the sense that is pertinent here, freedom is a mode of exerting one's will for the good of another—or all persons—and being open to persuasion or the leading of love and concern by others for oneself or for the group.

It is in this freedom that man turns and responds to the initiating love of God and seeks to embody that love in relationships. Through reciprocal release and guidance in corporate activities between God and man, and man and man, one moves toward mutuality or the development of value for oneself and for other persons. Life is, at the most basic level, a dynamic of leading and being led.

A. *The Dynamic at Work in the World*

In secular life we find many examples of leading and being led. The United States government, with its system of checks and balances, is one illustration. The President is the elected leader of the nation. His office directs and guides Congress and selects for appointment members of the judicial branch. Highly influential, both by the power of the office and by personal qualities of leadership, the President and his policies are shaped, governed, and finally—accepted, applied, amended, or rejected by the legislature, the courts, and the people themselves at the voting booths. The President not only affects, but is also affected by, the will of the people.

In the academic world, the figure of the excellent instructor or professor comes to mind. This individual imparts the knowledge of her chosen field, sharing and teaching from her personal perspective of truth. She elicits response, discussion, and contribution from her students to her knowledge. The professor offers insights, but receives insights as well from those she instructs, which substantiate, amplify, and challenge her own position.

The salesman who wishes to promote his product must be attuned to the needs and concerns of the prospective buyer. He cannot sell successfully to contrived or false needs; his sale must satisfy an existent need, whether or not that need had been openly recognized by the individual. A sale is constituted by the joint satisfaction of the seller and the buyer: the delivery of goods or services, and the reception and use of the goods or services by the satisfied customer.

Likewise, the management of family relations is a two-way street. Husband and wife guide one another; parents also influence and are influenced by their children. Not only do parents teach, instruct, and guide their offspring, the sons and daughters additionally expand, amend, and provide new areas to the knowledge of their mother and father. Acquisition and transmission of values flow from the mutual sharing and exploration of the whole family, generating a mutuality that grants to all members their personal integrity. The consideration of grandparents in this process only adds additional dimensions to the exchanges possible.

B. *The Dynamic at Work in Church Tradition*

When one turns to the pages of church tradition, instances of the interchange of leading and being led are most prevalent. One has only to study the christological debates of the first several centuries to find a relevant illustration. Origen, Basilides, Augustine, Pelagius, Athanasius, Arius, Clement of Alexandria, and Theodore of Mopsuestia formulated their doctrines of Christ in support of and in opposition to one another.

Beginning with the New Testament church and its remembrances and experiences of Jesus in the flesh, one thinker would add or change or restate the understanding of the nature of Christ, while another would refute and counterpropose. One, and then another, would move forward and then shift from the center to the fringes. The Chalcedonian definition was not the formulation of one individual or tradition. It incorporated various points of view, some of which had once been considered at odds with one another. The end-product of Chalcedon, when analyzed, reveals interaction or synthesis, creation and recreation —that is, the dynamic of leading and being led—made possible through the joint efforts of the orthodox and heretical.

The tradition of the church continues to the present day finding a focal expression in the activity of preaching. The minister or layperson by means of the sermon acquaints people with the foundations of the Christian faith and applies the scriptures and the words of the church fathers and others to modern-day situations and institutions. In doing this, one is being led by tradition as well as leading the tradition into new avenues of expression and interpretation. At this level, the dynamic is fostered and sustained by the relationship of minister and congregation wherein the minister addresses people from the insights and training of his life but is equally addressed by people speaking from the situations, needs, and experiences of their religious lives.

At the root of things the formation, promotion, and enlargement of church tradition is the experience of statement and restatement, of leading and being led, of action and reaction. Leadership is already established by the scriptures, by church documents, and especially, by the entities and understandings of Christ and the Holy Spirit. But this leadership is continually enlivened and witnessed to by the meanings it engenders in daily, ongoing life. The content and sources of the leadership, therefore, are led by new occasions to new expressions and perceptions. A nucleus of belief remains, yet it is a nucleus that develops and progresses in response to the ongoing creation of life by God and man.

C. *The Dynamic at Work in Scripture*

The New Testament most emphatically bears witness to the reflexive quality of leadership and direction. Paul, the apostle to the Gentiles, whose writings constitute a large segment of the New Testament canon, evidences some profound glimpses into this character of leadership.

Initially, it should be noted that the figure who urged that Christ's followers assume "compassion, kindness, lowliness, meekness, and patience; forbearing one another . . .

forgiving one another. . . And above all these, put on love" is the same individual who instructs persons "to teach and admonish one another" and also that they "do not quench the Spirit . . . but test everything." Guidance, as well as the activities of sustaining and supporting, is thus seen to be essential in Paul's concept of Christian life. Nowhere is this more clearly evident than in I Corinthians where the apostle himself details the character of love as patient, kind, and enduring. The reader finds that advice incapsulated in specific instructions to the Corinthians regarding food, marriage, and immorality.

More to the point is Paul's display of personal, theological, and ethical growth. In his early letters, this first century Christian evidences the view of an imminent end of the world, an end which he sees as coming in his own lifetime. By the time he wrote the later epistles, Christ's return no longer seems so near; things are very much different. Fellowship of the Christian with the Lord is not delayed or postponed until the Second Coming, nor even until resurrection immediately following physical death. This fellowship is enjoined in the here and now as one abides in Christ.

Likewise, the younger Paul plays down, if not actually negates, the value of family life. The apostle of First Corinthians stresses the advantages of the single and/or chaste life enjoining persons to remain in their current states in as pure a fashion as possible. Yet, in later years, on the occasion of his letter to the Colossians, Paul exhibits a differing valuation of interpersonal relationships. He urges an ethic of radical reciprocity and mutuality between husband and wife, parents and children, master and servant.

These changes and evidences of Paul's development do not proceed from impulsive conclusions or personal imbalance. The apostle is instead being led by the Holy Spirit, the image of Christ, personal experiences, and also by the experiences of his churches, to develop, explore, and amplify the details of his understanding. The apostle does not take a flat-footed stance and speak defensively; rather, Paul encounters and responds to his Lord and his parishioners in an ever-changing world in which mutuality is always possible.

Perhaps the most significant example of the dynamic of leading and being led, inasmuch as pastors and all Christians strive to model their ministries upon the example of Christ, is the story of Jesus and the woman of Canaan depicted in Matthew 15:22-28 (cf. Mark 7:24-30). The woman, who remains nameless, calls upon Jesus to cure her daughter. At first he gives no response, and then, when he finally speaks, he claims, "I was sent only to the lost sheep of the house of Israel." Yet the woman refuses to rest with this reply and entreats Jesus once again. This time, yielding to her implicit trust and confidence, Jesus asserts, "O woman, great is your faith! Be it done for you as you desire."

In its character, this story is unique in the Gospels. It is not that Jesus is elsewhere totally removed from the influence of others and the mutuality of interpersonal relationships; but rather, in this unusual and atypical exchange he is profoundly affected, perhaps even enlightened and instructed, by a Gentile woman! In the course of their encounter, he alters his concept, or at least the radius, of his ministry. The unparalleled teacher and leader of history is led and taught by the resilient faith of the foreigner; the integrity of Christ is deepened and enhanced by the objection of another.

D. *Claiming the Power of the Gospel*

In psychological terms, the method described here is that of effectance which guides individuals to creatively explore their capacities for influence and manipulation of, with, and against their environments. The counselor listens and moves on to direct the counselee in exploring conceptualities that afford a stable life. Theologically, this method speaks of leading persons to a life in Christ—to values and spiritual meaning, integration of faith and experience, and of thought and deed. The Christian, whether he or she be pastor or layperson, is undergirded by faith to envision and to guide persons in abundant life.

169

PASTORAL ASSERTIVENESS

Recent years have seen a trend and an emphasis on the psychological or theological professional being led by the other, whether counselee, parishioner, or society. The flow of exchange has been one-dimensional between the one in need and the one who addresses the need. We believe this trend, because it shortchanges the dynamic of leading and being led, is ultimately destructive and irresponsible, especially when practiced by those who rest their authority upon the gospel of Jesus Christ. The power of the gospel is denied when leadership, guidance, assertion, and direction are abdicated in favor of the leadings of culture or one's own sinful and self-serving desires.

By means of psychological theories and theological perspectives, and by examples of practical application, we urge and encourage the utilization of assertive leadership as a better way of pastoral care and counseling. Such a way claims and provides for the integrity of both counselor and counselee, of pastor and parishioner, in a mutual exchange.

Assertiveness is good. By an assertive person, we do not mean an autocrat, dictator, or conqueror. In counseling and leadership activities, one's integrity is always bound up in the integrity of other persons. Such is the import of the Second Commandment, "Love thy neighbor as thyself." Assertiveness and guidance are responsive and responsible uses of freedom to proclaim and instill the gospel in life.

Further, leading and being led means that the counselor or minister also develops in understanding, grasping, and embodying the content of the faith. One is not simply a force affecting others' lives; one's own life is affected by encounter with Christ and other persons. The relationship is well named by the word dynamic.

Ultimately, the impetus for Christian assertiveness and guidance is derived from scripture. The interrelatedness of Christ, the Holy Spirit, and he who would be a disciple of Christ is depicted in some of the most powerful words of the fourth gospel. It is the Spirit which convinces the world "of sin, righteousness, and of judgment," which guides individuals to the truth, and which bears witness to Christ even as individuals may bear that same witness. The power and influence assigned to the Holy Spirit by Christ is thus available and enjoined to the care and safekeeping of the Christian community.

Counseling and church leadership require that a stand be taken on the essence of truth and value in the gospel. A stance so grounded reveals itself in leading, guiding, and directing persons to the transformation of values and the creation of spiritual wholeness and meaning.

Pastoral assertiveness—grounded in the gospel of Jesus Christ, informed by the Holy Spirit, and directed to the physical, emotional, and spiritual welfare of oneself and others—is truly pastoral care.

NOTES

CHAPTER 1

1. Seward Hiltner, *Preface to Pastoral Theology* (Nashville: Abingdon Press, 1958). This essay is the fullest exposition of the ministries of healing, sustaining, and guiding. Later treatments as found in William Clebsch and Charles Jaekle, *Pastoral Care in Historical Perspective* (Englewood Cliffs, N.J.: Prentice-Hall, 1964), and Don S. Browning, *The Moral Context of Pastoral Care* (Philadelphia: The Westminster Press, 1976) are of further assistance in developing a systematic understanding of the primary ways in which pastoral care contributes to ministerial formation and practice.

CHAPTER 2

1. White's research and contributions to the field of psychology range from work in *Abnormal Psychology* to his charting of healthy personality development in *Lives in Progress.* Of special interest is his paper, "Motivation Reconsidered: The Concept of Competence" (*Psychological Review,* 66 [1959]), now a classic statement in the field of developmental psychology.

2. Robert W. White, "Ego and Reality in Psychoanalytic Theory," in *Psychological Issues,* Vol. III (New York: International Universities Press, 1963), pp. 34-35.

3. Some of the standard works in the field include David K. Switzer, *The Minister as Crisis Counselor* (Nashville: Abingdon Press, 1974); Arlene Carmen and Howard Moody, *Abortion Counseling and Social Change* (Valley Forge, Pa.: Judson Press, 1973); Edgar Draper, *Psychiatry and Pastoral Care* (Englewood Cliffs, N.J.: Prentice-Hall, 1965); Harold I. Haas, *Pastoral Counseling with People in Distress* (St. Louis: Concordia Publishing House, 1970); Wayne Oates, *Pastoral Care and Counseling in Grief and Separation* (Philadelphia: Fortress Press, 1976); *Pastoral Care in Crucial Human Situations,* ed. Wayne Oates and Andrew Lester (Valley Forge, Pa.:

Judson Press, 1969); Thomas A. Shipp, *Helping the Alcoholic and His Family* (Englewood Cliffs, N.J.: Prentice-Hall, 1963); Charles Stewart, *The Minister as Marriage Counselor,* rev. ed. (Nashville: Abingdon Press, 1970); Howard W. Stone, *Crisis Counseling* (Philadelphia: Fortress Press, 1976).

CHAPTER 3

1. To explore the theoretical issues involved in this argument, see chapter 7 for a detailed discussion of the psychological dynamics common to psychotherapy and selling.

2. For more complete development of this position, see Seward Hiltner, *Preface to Pastoral Theology* (Nashville: Abingdon Press, 1958), chapters 1 and 4, especially the footnote discussion: "Pastoral theology must have full commerce with every discipline that is studying shepherding [caring]. And every bit of relevant insight it discovers about shepherding, regardless of source, must be considered in the light of its theological significance" (p. 220). We claim that the selling model offers relevant insight about pastoral care, and especially pastoral assertiveness, that has direct and explicit theological significance.

CHAPTER 5

1. Rollo May, *Power and Innocence* (New York: W. W. Norton, 1972), chapter 9.

2. Don S. Browning, *Generative Man: Psychoanalytic Perspectives* (Philadelphia: The Westminster Press, 1973), chapter 7.

CHAPTER 6

1. Keith Bridston, *Church Politics* (New York: World Publishing Co., 1969). This Lutheran pastor, theologian, and church politician openly advocated this approach several years ago. It is a philosophy we endorse and applaud both for opening up political realities by making church elections less covert *and* to encourage pastors to be less conflicted about their leadership aspirations.

2. Browning, *Generative Man,* pp. 212 ff. The perspective preferred by Browning is clearly similar to that of Erik Erikson who wrote, "Truly worthwhile acts enhance a mutuality between the doer and the other—a mutuality which strengthens the doer even as it strengthens the other" (cf. Erikson, *Insight and Responsibility: Lectures on the Ethical Implications of Psychoanalytic Insight* [New York: W. W. Norton, 1964], p. 233).

CHAPTER 7

1. Calvin Hall and Gardner Lindzey, *Theories of Personality,* 2d ed. (New York: John Wiley & Sons, 1970), presents a comprehensive introduction to the dominant personality theories and therapy models of today.

173

2. Erik Erikson, "Identity and the Life Cycle: Selected Papers," *Psychological Issues,* Vol. I (New York: International Universities Press, 1959), see chapter 1 especially.

3. Carl R. Rogers, *On Becoming a Person* (Boston: Houghton Mifflin, 1961), p. 37.

4. Carl R. Rogers, *Client-Centered Therapy* (Boston: Houghton Mifflin, 1951), p. 163.

5. *Ibid.*

6. *Ibid.,* p. 162.

7. Howard J. Clinebell, *Basic Types of Pastoral Counseling* (Nashville: Abingdon Press, 1966).

8. Erikson, *Insight and Responsibility: Lectures on the Ethical Implications of Psychoanalytic Insight* (New York: W. W. Norton, 1964), p. 233.

9. Rogers, *On Becoming a Person,* p. 67.

10. Clinebell, *Basic Types,* p. 85.

11. *Ibid.*

12. *Ibid.,* p. 86.

13. *Ibid.*

14. Rogers, *Client-Centered Therapy,* p. 194.

15. Clinebell, *Basic Types,* p. 86.

16. *Ibid.*

17. Rogers, *Client-Centered Therapy,* p. 203.

CHAPTER 9

1. Philip Rieff, *The Triumph of the Therapeutic: Uses of Faith After Freud* (New York: Harper Torch Books, 1968), especially chapter 8.

CHAPTER 11

1. Charles Hartshorne, *The Divine Relativity* (New Haven: Yale University Press, 1948).

2. Seward Hiltner, *Preface to Pastoral Theology.*

3. Henri J. M. Nouwen, *The Living Reminder* (New York: The Seabury Press, 1977), p. 63.

4. Don S. Browning, *The Moral Context of Pastoral Care* (Philadelphia: The Westminster Press, 1976), especially his concept of practical rationality.

5. Nouwen, *Living Reminder,* p. 64.